101
Clear Grammar
TESTS

Reproducible Grammar Tests for ESL/EFL Classes

Keith S. Folse

Jeanine Ivone

Shawn Pollgreen

Ann Arbor

THE UNIVERSITY OF MICHIGAN PRESS

To the Teacher

101 Clear Grammar Tests is a set of 101 reproducible (photocopiable) tests on common grammar points covered in beginning, intermediate, and advanced ESL grammar books. The tests in this book are intended to accompany *Clear Grammar 1, 2, 3,* and *4.* However, in actuality, the tests are suitable for use with any beginning to advanced ESL grammar book or series.

Each grammar point has two tests devoted to it. For example, Test 49 and Test 50 cover phrasal verbs, and Test 79 and Test 80 cover noun clauses.

Some of the benefits of having multiple tests available for teachers (and learners) include:

❶ teachers can find a test that resembles their own teaching style;

❷ teachers can find a test that resembles the way the learners expect to be tested;

❸ teachers can use one test as a practice test and still have one for the actual test;

❹ learners can see their progress in various ways because the tests use a variety of question types;

❺ learners learn in different ways with different styles, so tests with different kinds of questions are a good thing; and

❻ learners can have a second (or third) chance with a grammar point if the teacher permits this.

It should be noted that the tests included in this book were submitted by three different instructors with three different writing styles, three teaching styles, and three testing variations. The reason for this number of authors was to intentionally produce a book of tests that would include a variety of *types* of questions as well as *approaches* to testing. In many ways, the 101 tests in the book are different, but in many ways they are also similar.

There is no one who knows your teaching situation and your learners better than you do, so it is up to you to choose testing materials that match not only what has been taught—that is, the content—but also the way in which the students were taught—for example, drill, conversation, writing—and the way in which the students are accustomed to being tested. While experimentation and innovation are appropriate to the classroom at the right times, learners under the stress of a testing situation may not do well on tests that are outside of what they are expecting.

We have tried to include a wide array of types of questions in the tests. Examples include matching, multiple choice, error location, error correction, completion (filling in the blanks), connecting sentence parts, rearranging word order, grammatical identification (e.g., *underline the correct words to complete each sentence*), and manipulation (e.g., *write the correct possessive form*). It is important for teachers to make sure that their students are familiar with and as comfortable as possible with the types of questions used in the test. Students may have problems answering a question because they do not know the answer, but they should not have problems answering the question because of the question itself.

For teachers' convenience, there are three ways to access a test for a given grammar point.

1. If you are using the *Clear Grammar* series, simply look for the book and unit number in the Contents. For example, if you want to test Unit 4 from Book 2, you would look through the Contents for that unit number in that particular book. The appropriate tests for Unit 4 in Book 2 are Test 29 and Test 30.

2. If you want a test on a specific grammar point but are not using the *Clear Grammar* series, you should look for the name of the grammar point in the Contents. For example, if you want a test on articles, you would look down the listing of grammatical points until you find the term *articles*. The appropriate tests for articles are Test 25 and Test 26.

3. A third way to access a test on a given grammar point is to use the index at the back of the book. If you want a test on prepositions, you would look through the alphabetized list until you find the term *prepositions*, and then you will find that Test 21, Test 22, Test 55, Test 56, Test 57, Test 58, Test 87, and Test 88 deal with this particular grammar point.

Book Organization

- *Tests 1–24* cover Book 1, which is beginning level.
- *Tests 25–48* cover Book 2, which is high-beginning level
- *Tests 49–70* cover Book 3, which is low-intermediate to intermediate level.
- *Tests 71–92* cover Book 4, which is high-intermediate to low-advanced level.
- *Tests 93–101* cover all types of ESL grammar problems and are advanced. Because these tests do not focus on only one grammar point, they require students to review many points simultaneously, thus testing editing skills as well.

Contents

The following listing gives the test number, the corresponding volume (book) number and unit number from the *Clear Grammar* series, and a description of the grammar point(s).

Name _____   Date _____

Part A Fill in the blanks with the correct form of *be*. (If the sentence is negative [neg], write the negative form of *be*.)

Example: David ___is not___ from the United States [neg].

1. The Earth ___is___ a large planet.

2. Two students in this class ___are___ from Venezuela.

3. A banana ___isn't___ a vegetable [neg].

4. Some snakes ___are___ dangerous animals.

5. I ___am___ happy to be in the United States.

6. Mexico ___isn't___ a part of the United States [neg].

7. Bill Clinton ___is___ a former president of the United States.

8. Tom Cruise and Nicole Kidman ___are___ famous actors.

9. Florida and Georgia ___aren't___ in the Northeast [neg].

10. I ___m not___ from Ukraine [neg].

Part B Read the words, and then make a question. In the blank below the question, write a short answer. Remember to use periods (.) and question marks (?).

Example: the car outside is   *Is the car outside?*

Yes, it is.

1. the stars sky in the are   Are the stars in the sky?

   yes, they are.

2. Canada in United States the is   Is Canada in the united states?

   yes, it is.

3. you are student a   Are you a student.

   yes, I am

4. Paris the capital France is of   Is paris the capital of france?

   yes, it is.

5. necessary school is   Is school necessary?

   yes, it is.

6. animals dogs are   Are dogs animals?

   yes, they are.

7. blue the is sky   *Is the sky blue?*
                      Yes, it is.

8. English native your language is   *Is it your native language?*
                                      Yes it is.

9. flat the world is   *Is the world flat?*

10. your parents are in U.S. the   *Are your parents in the U.S*

Part C Fill in the blanks with the correct subject pronoun: *I, you, he, she, it, we, they.*

1. My mother is in the kitchen. _____*She*_____ is cooking dinner.

2. Juan is a student in our class. _____*He*_____ sits behind me.

3. My favorite ice cream is chocolate. _____*It*_____ love chocolate ice cream!

4. Nancy and Jenny went to the store. _____*They*_____ need to buy some clothes.

5. This car is very old. _____*it*_____ needs a lot of work.

6. You and I both need help in grammar, so _____*We*_____ can ask the teacher.

7. Fred's sister is very funny! _____*She*_____ tells great jokes.

8. Lisa's son is three years old, and _____*He*_____ is very smart.

9. When my parents want to talk to me, _____*they*_____ call me on the phone.

10. My best friend and I love to dance. _____*We*_____ dance as often as possible.

TEST 2 Present Tense of *Be*

Clear Grammar 1, Unit 1

Name _____   Date _____

Part A Circle the letter of the answer that correctly completes each sentence.

1. Jeff _____. He _____ at a meeting with bank representatives.

   (A) are in Chicago . . . is   (C) is in Chicago . . . is

   (B) in Chicago . . . are   (D) is Chicago . . . are

2. Starting your own business _____ easy.

   (A) is not   (C) are not

   (B) no is   (D) no are

3. He _____ about taking risks with his money.

   (A) are nervous   (C) nervous

   (B) is nervous   (D) am nervous

4. _____ in her husband's plans?

   (A) Are Charlotte interested   (C) Charlotte are interested

   (B) Is Charlotte interested   (D) Charlotte is interested

5. Local investors _____ prepared to lend her money.

   (A) are   (C) is

   (B) am   (D) be

6. His parents _____ another city.

   (A) am in   (C) in am

   (B) is in   (D) are in

7. _____ proud of their son?

   (A) They are   (C) Are they

   (B) Is they   (D) They am

8. John and his wife _____ sure that they are making a good decision.

   (A) no are   (C) no am

   (B) are not   (D) not am

9. _____ located in a busy area of town?

    (A) Is the store   (C) The store is

    (B) The store are   (D) Are the store

10. There _____ another shoe store within five miles of his store.

    (A) no is   (C) no are

    (B) is not   (D) are not

Part B Look at the underlined part of each sentence. If the underlined part is correct, circle C. If it is wrong, circle X, and write the correct form on the line. Six of the sentences are wrong.

C   X   1.   Julia and Benjamin <u>are</u> married. _____

C   X   2.   <u>My sister and I are</u> in a restaurant. _____

C   X   3.   The <u>sky are</u> not clear today.   *is* _____

C   X   4.   Canada <u>aren't</u> in the United States. *isn't* _____

C   X   5.   *Q:* "Is the weather nice today?" *A:* "<u>Yes, is.</u>" *it* _____

C   X   6.   Clearwater <u>is</u> on the west coast of Florida. _____

C   X   7.   The boats on the water <u>is</u> large. *are* _____

C   X   8.   The beaches in California <u>am</u> not cold. *are* _____

C   X   9.   Jenny's mother and father <u>are</u> in Virginia. _____

C   X   10.   <u>This car is</u> yours? _____

                 Is this car yours?

TEST 3   Present Tense of Regular Verbs

Clear Grammar 1, Unit 2

Name _____   Date _____

Part A   Circle the correct form of each verb.

1. Henry (**likes**, like) to watch football on television.

2. Ben (play, **plays**) hockey every winter.

3. Renee (knows not, **doesn't know**) how to speak German.

4. Angie and Chris (don't lives, **don't live**) in New York.

5. When you (**get**, gets) home, (**call**, calls) me.

6. I (**go**, goes) to the movies every weekend.

7. Marsha (**doesn't listen**, doesn't listens) to country music.

8. Fred (have, **has**) a sailboat that he (**sails**, sail) on Saturday.

9. Does Vincent (practices, **practice**) piano every day?

10. Ellen and Gina (eats, **eat**) sushi as often as they can.

Part B   Write the correct words on the lines. Follow the example.

Example: (want) __Do__ you __want__ to go to the party?

1. (sell) ___Do___ Wal-Mart ___sell___ bicycles?

2. (speak) ___Do___ you ___speak___ English?

3. (study) ___Do___ you ___study___ every day?

4. (enjoy) ___Do___ you ___enjoy___ reading?

5. (need) ___Do___ your friend ___need___ help with her homework?

6. (want) ___Does___ your sister ___want___ you to visit her?

7. (call) ___Do___ you ___call___ your parents often?

8. (teach) ___Does___ your teacher ___teach___ Spanish?

9. (drink) ___Do___ you ___drink___ coffee?

10. (have) ___Does___ your sister ___have___ other children?

Part C Circle the letter of the answer that correctly completes each sentence.

1. _____ to travel?

   (A) You like   (C) Like you

   (B) Are you like   (D) Do you like

2. Are you from the United States? _____

   (A) No, I'm not.   (C) No, I don't.

   (B) No, she doesn't.   (D) No, she isn't.

3. _____ horror novels?

   (A) Do your sister read   (C) Does your sister read

   (B) Does your sister reads   (D) Is your sister read

4. Is your mother in this country? _____

   (A) Yes, she does.   (C) No, she doesn't.

   (B) Yes, she is.   (D) Yes, she isn't.

5. _____ play basketball?

   (A) Does your brothers   (C) Do your brother

   (B) Is your brother   (D) Does your brother

6. Do you like to do homework? _____

   (A) No, I don't.   (C) No, I don't like.

   (B) No, I'm not.   (D) Yes, I like.

7. _____ your parents _____ you e-mail?

   (A) Does . . . write   (C) Do . . . write

   (B) Does . . . writes   (D) Do . . . writes

8. Nancy _____ in Virginia.

   (A) live   (C) is lives

   (B) lives   (D) does lives

9. _____ you _____ how to ski?

   (A) Do . . . know   (C) Does . . . know

   (B) Do . . . knows   (D) Does . . . knows

10. Rachel _____ to go to the doctor.

   (A) no wants   (C) don't want

   (B) doesn't want   (D) wants not

TEST 4 Present Tense of Regular Verbs

Clear Grammar 1, Unit 2

Name _____   Date _____

Part A Use the words to make statements and questions with the present tense of the verbs. Follow the example.

Example: you and your parents / (travel) / a lot _Do you and your parents travel a lot?_

1. our family / (eat) / dinner / at 6:00 _Does our family eat dinner at 6.00?_
2. chefs / (cook) / in restaurants _Do chefs cook in restaurants?_
3. pandas / (live) / in China _Do pandas live in China?_
4. birds / (fly) / south / for the winter _Do birds fly south for the winter?_
5. Florida / (have) / a lot of rain / in the summer _Does Florida have_
6. you and your roommate / (study) / together _Do you and your roommate s?_
7. your class / (begin) / at 9:00 _Does your class begin_ ?
8. Terry / (understand) / French _Does Terry_ .
9. Dean / (watch) / television / every day _Does_ .
10. Martha / (speak) / English _Does_ ?

Part B Fill in the blanks with the present tense form of the verbs. Make each sentence negative. Follow the example.

Example: (like) Billy _doesn't like_ to play basketball.

1. (leave)   The waiters _don't leave_ the restaurant until all the customers are gone.
2. (do)   Leslie _doesn't do_ her homework carefully.
3. (begin)   School _doesn't begin_ until September.
4. (play)   The little girls _don't_ with the little boys.
5. (take)   John and Jim _don't_ the bus home from school.
6. (use)   Most animals _don't_ tools to perform tasks.
7. (think)   We _don't_ we're ready for the test.
8. (work)   Many writers _don't_ in an office.
9. (make)   Alfred _doesn't_ breakfast for himself before he leaves the house.
10. (call)   Steve feels badly because he _does_ his mother every week.

Part C Fill in the blanks with *do, does, don't,* or *doesn't.*

1. The sun ___doesn't___ revolve around the earth.

2. ___Do___ you and your friends like to dance?

3. Dogs ___doesn't___ like to take baths.

4. ___Does___ summer follow winter?

5. My brother ___doesn't___ know how to cook.

6. My classmates ___don't___ understand the lesson.

7. ___Does___ this street lead to the theater?

8. ___Do___ politicians tell the truth?

9. The teacher ___doesn't___ have our test results yet.

10. The flowers in my garden ___don't___ seem to be growing.

TEST 5 Demonstratives
(*this, that, these, those*)

Clear Grammar 1, Unit 3

Name _____   Date _____

Part A Write *this, that, these,* or *those* on the lines. Follow the examples.

Examples: (here) _*This*_ cat is fat.

(there) _*That*_ cat is skinny.

1. (here)   ___these___ students understand the lesson.
2. (there)   ___Those___ students don't need help.
3. (here)   Does ___this___ jacket belong to you?
4. (there) Are ___those___ books yours?
5. (here)   ___This___ pencil is mine.
6. (there)   ___Those___ pencils are yours.
7. (here)   ___This___ class is interesting.
8. (there)   ___That___ dog doesn't have a home.
9. (here)   ___This___ pen doesn't work.
10. (there) Does ___That___ girl look familiar to you?
11. (here)   Is ___this___ car expensive?
12. (there)   ___Those___ children are young.
13. (here)   ___This___ movie is boring.
14. (here)   ___This___ cake is delicious!
15. (there)   ___that___ tree is huge!

Part B Read each sentence carefully. Look at the underlined part. If the underlined part is correct, circle C. If it is wrong, circle X, and write the correct form on the line. Eight sentences are not correct.

C   X   1. *These* This are easy exercises. (here) _____

C   X   2. *These* That are Italian shoes. (here) _____

C   X   3. Those are expensive houses. (there) _____

C   X   4. *These* This are playful puppies. (here) _____

C   X   5. This is a great day to go to the beach. (here) _____

C   X   6. Is this *that* an easy subject for you? (there) _____

C   X   7. This is delicious coffee. (here) _____

C   X   8. *those* That are my eyeglasses. (there) _____

C   X   9. *That* Those is Gloria's soda. (there) _____

C   X   10. These are challenging questions. (here) _____

C   X   11. *that* Those is a good idea! (there) _____

C   X   12. Are those your pens? (there) _____

C   X   13. *This* That is an interesting book. (here) _____

C   X   14. That is a fluffy cloud. (there) _____

C   X   15. Is that the right time on the clock? (there) _____

TEST 6 Demonstratives

(*this, that, these, those*)

Clear Grammar 1, Unit 3

Name _____   Date _____

Part A Circle the word that correctly completes each sentence.

1. I am happy I bought (this, these) video. (Those, This) is my favorite movie!

2. (Those, That) shoes are pretty. Where did you get them?

3. Before we go to sleep, we need to wash (that, these) dishes.

4. There's an umbrella over there. Is (this, that) yours?

5. (This, That) is going to be a good day. I slept well last night, and I ate a good breakfast this morning.

6. The students asked to leave early, but the teacher disagreed with (those, that) idea.

7. (These, This) cookies are easy to bake.

8. I want to try on (this, those) shirts I saw at the mall last week.

9. What kind of tree is (this, that) over there?

10. (That, Those) hockey players won the championship game.

11. When I finish (these, this) book, I'm going to see the movie.

12. My dog is barking at (this, that) cat over there.

13. Can you help me, please? I'm going to drop (those, these) books!

14. The police are asking (these, those) people across the street about the accident.

15. (This, That) restaurant we just passed is excellent. You should go there some day.

Part B Circle the letter of the answer that correctly completes each sentence. Pay attention to the word in parentheses.

1. (there) Is _____ knife sharp enough to cut the meat?

   (A) this   (C) these

   (B) that   (D) those

2. (here) _____ are challenging questions.

   (A) This   (C) These

   (B) That   (D) Those

3. (there) Do you know _____ people?

   (A) this   (C) these

   (B) that   (D) those

4. (here) _____ is an inexpensive necklace.

   (A) This   (C) These

   (B) That   (D) Those

5. (there) _____ airplane is making a lot of noise.

   (A) This   (C) These

   (B) That   (D) Those

6. (here) _____ are easy recipes to follow.

   (A) This   (C) These

   (B) That   (D) Those

7. (there) _____ doctors operated on my father.

   (A) This   (C) These

   (B) That   (D) Those

8. (here) _____ is a comfortable robe.

   (A) This   (C) These

   (B) That   (D) Those

9. (there) Will you give me _____ book, please?

   (A) this   (C) these

   (B) that   (D) those

10. (here) _____ are extra disks. Do you want them?

    (A) This   (C) These

    (B) That   (D) Those

11. (there) _____ is an excellent idea! We should go away for the weekend!

    (A) This   (C) These

    (B) That   (D) Those

12. (here) Do you want to eat _____ carrots? If not, I'm going to throw them away.

    (A) this   (C) these

    (B) that   (D) those

13. (there) _____ giraffes are beautiful animals.

    (A) This   (C) These

    (B) That   (D) Those

14. (here) I can't finish _____ cake. You can eat the rest of it.

    (A) this   (C) these

    (B) that   (D) those

15. (there) _____ was a funny story my grandmother told us last night!

    (A) This   (C) These

    (B) That   (D) Those

TEST 7 Possessive Adjectives (*my, your,* etc.)

Clear Grammar 1, Unit 4

Name _____   '   Date _____

Part A Underline the correct word to complete each sentence.

1. Linda is from Florida. Sailing is (her, she) favorite sport.

2. (I, My) love to watch old movies. (I, My) favorite one is *The Miracle Worker.*

3. Does (you, your) mother speak English?

4. (He, His) sings very well. (His, He) prefers to sing country music.

5. My best friend is from Italy. (Her, She) name is Elena.

6. I think my dog is sick. (Its, It) nose is dry.

7. We don't have a lot of time. (Our, We) final exam is next week!

8. If you and your best friend want to come over, (your, you) can.

9. The stars are bright tonight. (They, Their) look beautiful against the black sky.

10. Martin is happy because (he, his) got a bicycle for (he, his) birthday.

Part B Read each sentence. If it is correct, write C in the box. If it is wrong, write X in the box, and write the sentence again to make it correct. Six of the sentences are not correct.

1. [X] Do you like your apartment?

   _____

2. [ ] Susan and her sister are twins. They look exactly alike.

   _____

3. [ ] Kim is tired because her children are sick.

   _____

4. [X] Our teacher sits behind she desk every day.   *her*

   _____

5. [ ] Michael called her daughter to see if she is home.

   _____

6. ☑ My cat is sleeping in their bed. (The bed belongs to the cat.)

_____

7. ☑ Henry's office is in Washington. He is a lawyer.

_____

their
8. ☒ Sarah and Brett are rich. They house is big.

_____

they
9. ☒ Fred and Louise live in Miami. Their like hot weather.

_____

10. ☑ Prince Charles is the queen's son. He lives in Buckingham Palace.

_____

Part C Fill in the blanks with the correct possessive adjective.

1. If you and your husband need money, _____their_____ bank can lend you some.

2. When Fred bought _____his_____ house, he made a 20 percent deposit.

3. This table is broken. _____Its_____ legs are shaky.

4. The teenagers had a party because _____their_____ parents were out of town.

5. My family is excited because _____they_____ trip to Paris is in two days.

6. Peggy is at home with _____his_____ family.

7. If Christopher sells _____his_____ car, he can afford to buy a newer one.

8. I don't know what to do about _____His_____ father's health problems.

9. You and your family may need to paint _____our_____ house in a few months.

10. Oliver went to the park with _____his_____ dog.

TEST 8 Possessive Adjectives
(*my, your,* etc.)

Clear Grammar 1, Unit 4

Name _____   Date _____

Part A   Circle the letter of the answer that correctly completes each sentence.

1. Do you want to borrow _____ pencil?

   (A) your   (C) my

   (B) its   (D) I

2. I didn't bring _____ book to class. Will you share _____ book with me?

   (A) my . . . your   (C) me . . . her

   (B) I . . . his   (D) my . . . our

3. The president of the company spoke to _____ employees about _____ salary.

   (A) them . . . our   (C) their . . . his

   (B) his . . . their   (D) him . . . its

4. My grandmother calls _____ brother every week.

   (A) his   (C) her

   (B) she   (D) their

5. The horse hurt _____ leg when it tried to jump over the puddle.

   (A) their   (C) your

   (B) its   (D) our

6. All of _____ neighbors try to keep _____ neighborhood clean.

   (A) his . . . her   (C) your . . . its

   (B) your . . . his   (D) my . . . our

7. Do you and _____ sister go to the same school?

   (A) your   (C) its

   (B) you   (D) our

8. My parents sold _____ house and bought a condominium.

   (A) your   (C) their

   (B) her   (D) its

9. I asked _____ doctor for medicine for bad headaches.

    (A) its   (C) mine

    (B) my   (D) I

10. _____ sister and I had a party for _____ brother.

    (A) I . . . his   (C) Your . . . him

    (B) My . . . our   (D) My . . . her

11. _____ teacher introduced us to _____ daughter.

    (A) Our . . . its   (C) Your . . . she

    (B) Their . . . my   (D) Our . . . her

12. When do you plan to earn _____ college degree?

    (A) your   (C) my

    (B) their   (D) his

13. Bradley did well on _____ final exam.

    (A) her   (C) his

    (B) my   (D) him

14. People like to have _____ work appreciated by others.

    (A) his   (C) her

    (B) my   (D) their

15. Maria washed _____ face before she went to bed.

    (A) my   (C) her

    (B) its   (D) his

Part B Underline the correct possessive adjective in each sentence.

1. Snakes lose (its, their) skin every year.

2. When did you and (your, its) family leave (their, your) country?

3. I fed (its, my) cat before I left the house.

4. What is (your, you) middle name?

5. My husband and I have to share a car because (me, my) car is in the shop.

6. Dave wrote (her, his) first book in 2003.

7. A lion will do anything to protect (your, its) cubs from danger.

8. I need to cut (my, its) grass before the weekend is over.

9. The young couple announced (her, their) plans to get married.

10. Do you have (your, its) driver's license with you?

11. My roommate and I are trying to sell (our, we) furniture.

12. The professional diver hit (his, him) head on the diving board.

13. Where did you put (your, you) watch?

14. My mother won't tell anyone (his, her) recipe for lasagna.

15. Do you want to come to (us, our) house for dinner next week?

TEST 9 Past Tense of *Be*

Clear Grammar 1, Unit 5

Name _____   Date _____

Part A Fill in the blanks with the correct form of *be*.

1. When David _____ was _____ a little boy, he liked to play outside.

2. The people in the crowd _____ were _____ excited about seeing Celine Dion last night.

3. Jan _____ was _____ not happy about the low grade she got on her test.

4. _____ Was _____ your teacher in class yesterday?

5. The movie we saw last night _____ was _____ a long one; it lasted three hours!

6. My sister and brother _____ were _____ in their rooms when my mother got home.

7. _____ were _____ you good at math when you _____ were _____ a child?

8. The mother dog tried to feed her puppies, but they _____ were _____ not hungry, so they didn't eat.

9. _____ were _____ you nervous when you first arrived in this country?

10. There _____ was _____ no milk in the refrigerator, so T.J. didn't eat cereal for breakfast.

Part B Read each sentence carefully. Look at the underlined part. If the underlined part is correct, circle C. If it is wrong, circle X, and write the correct form on the line. Six sentences are not correct.

C   X   1.   Yesterday <u>is</u> a very cold day!

_____ was _____

C   X   2.   Fred loved to race cars when he <u>is</u> younger.

_____ was _____

C   X   3.   These days I <u>am</u> confident in my ability to learn English.

_____ am _____

C   X   4.   The United States <u>was</u> located south of Canada.

_____

C   X   5.   Both Teddy and Franklin Roosevelt <u>was</u> Presidents.

_____ were _____

C   X   6.   Ronald Reagan <u>was</u> President for eight years.

_____

C   X   7.   <u>Am</u> your family large or small?

_____

C   X   8.   <u>Were</u> you at home last night?

_____

C   X   9.   The students in the class <u>were</u> nervous about tomorrow's test.

_____

C   X   10.   Look! There <u>is</u> a white dog outside!

_____

Part C Use the words to make past tense questions with *be*. Remember to use question marks.

Example: the plane / on time / (be)   *Was the plane on time?*

1. you / tired / (be) *Were you tired?*

2. he / at home / (be) / when you called *Was he at home when you called*

3. Julia Roberts / in the movie / (be) *Was J. in the movie*

4. it / hot / (be) / last week *Was it hot last week.*

5. you / on the train / (be) / for a long time _____

6. she / in your group / (be) _____

7. your friends / at the party / (be) _____

8. the concert / good / (be) _____

9. these cookies / difficult to make / (be) _____

10. your mother / surprised to see you / (be) _____

TEST 10 Past Tense of *Be*

Clear Grammar 1, Unit 5

Name _____   Date _____

Part A Circle the letter of the answer that correctly completes each sentence.

1. _____ visible last night?

    (A) The moon was   (C) Was the moon

    (B) The moon is   (D) Is the moon

2. _____ three hours long.

    (A) Was the movie   (C) The movie was

    (B) Did the movie   (D) The movie were

3. _____ in class when we arrived.

    (A) Was the teacher   (C) Did the teacher

    (B) The teacher wasn't   (D) The teacher weren't

4. *Q:* "Were you at your friend's house last night?"

    A: "Yes, _____."

    (A) you were   (C) I were

    (B) I did   (D) I was

5. _____ your favorite book when you _____ a child?

    (A) What was . . . were   (C) What were . . . was

    (B) What did . . . were   (D) What were . . . were

6. The children _____ because they ate a lot of candy.

    (A) no were hungry   (C) hungry were not

    (B) weren't hungry   (D) isn't hungry

7. The water _____ too cold, so we didn't go swimming.

    (A) is   (C) was

    (B) were   (D) are

8. *Q:* "_____ the movie theater full when you arrived?"

    A: "No, _____."

    (A) Were . . . it wasn't   (C) Was . . . it did

    (B) Was . . . it wasn't   (D) Were . . . it was

9. There _____ many kinds of desserts on the menu.

    (A) is   (C) was

    (B) no were   (D) were

10. Rachel and Emily _____ about going to the concert.

    (A) excited were   (C) was excited

    (B) were excited   (D) didn't were excited

Part B Underline the word or words that correctly complete each sentence.

1. I (am, was) tired, so I went to sleep early last night.

2. The painters (was not, were not) finished painting when I got home.

3. The students (is not, were not) happy about their homework assignment.

4. (Did, Were) your parents at the airport when you left your country?

5. (Was, Did) the test difficult?

6. When (did, were) you born?

7. The mother duck (was, were) with her baby ducks near the lake.

8. I (was, were) in the pool when it started to rain.

9. My best friend and I (was, were) hungry, so we went to a sushi restaurant.

10. (Were, Was) there anything good on television last night?

Part C Read each sentence carefully. If the sentence is correct, circle C. If it is wrong, circle X, and write the correct answer on the line. Seven of the sentences are not correct.

C   X   1.   The senators was in a meeting until 5:30 last night. _____ *were*

C   X   2.   My grass were brown, so I put water on it. _____

C   X   3.   There were a lot of people in line at the grocery store._____ *are*

C   X   4.   Rose is born in 1930._____

C   X   5.   Both candidates were late for the mayoral debate. _____

C   X   6.   California isn't a state in 1776. _____

C   X   7.   Tom and Nicole didn't together in 1985._____

C   X   8.   The housekeepers isn't at work yesterday._____ *weren't*

C   X   9.   The sky wasn't clear, so we couldn't see the shuttle. _____

C   X   10. Texas was a hot state. _____ *is*

TEST 11 Past Tense of Regular and Irregular Verbs

Clear Grammar 1, Unit 6

Name _____   Date _____

Part A Circle the letter of the answer that correctly completes each sentence.

1. Nina _____ to go to Virginia.

   (A) didn't wanted   (C) didn't want

   (B) wanted not   (D) doesn't wanted

2. Nancy _____ the dishes before she went to bed.

   (A) did wash   (C) was washed

   (B) washed   (D) was wash

3. _____ a chance to see the lunar eclipse?

   (A) You did get   (C) Did you got

   (B) You got   (D) Did you get

4. The teacher _____ the blackboard before she _____ the room.

   (A) was erased . . . left   (C) erased . . . left

   (B) were erased . . . leaved   (D) erases . . . leaved

5. The cashier _____ the numbers together and _____ us our total.

   (A) adds . . . gave   (C) adds . . . was gave

   (B) added . . . gives   (D) added . . . gave

6. _____ candy when you were little?

   (A) Do you like   (C) Did you like

   (B) Liked you   (D) You liked

7. I _____ my shirt before I put it on.

   (A) was ironed   (C) were ironed

   (B) ironed   (D) irons

8. Elias and Ben _____ outside for hours.

   (A) played   (C) plays

   (B) plaid   (D) are played

9. _____ to Switzerland last summer?

(A) Did you go   (C) Did you went

(B) Do you go   (D) Do you went

10. I _____ English in my country.

(A) am studied   (C) studied

(B) studyed   (D) was studied

Part B Write the correct words to complete each sentence. Be sure to use the past tense.

Example: (go) *John:* ___*Did you go*___ to your friend's house yesterday?

   Jim: No, I ___*didn't*___ . I ___*went*___ to the library.

1. (visit) *Mark:* _____ the Sistine Chapel

   when you went to Italy?

   Jenny: No, _____. I didn't have enough time.

2. (clean) *Norma:* _____ Margaret _____ the house before

   she left?

   Liz: Yes, _____. All the dishes are clean.

3. (pass) *Albert:* _____ the exam?

   Barry: No, she _____. She failed.

4. (cook) *Beth:*   _____ your mother _____ dinner for you?

   Susan: No, _____. I _____ dinner

   for myself.

5. (rain) *Bob:*   _____ it _____ this morning?

   Dan: Yes, _____, but it _____ last night.

6. (think) *Sarah:* _____ you _____ about your answer before

   you spoke?

   Kim: Yes, _____ a lot about what I should say.

7. (drink) *Tony:*   _____ Lance _____ enough water before

   the race?

   Nina: Yes, _____. _____ three glasses.

8. (listen) *Charlie:* _____ you _____ to the radio before you

   went to sleep?

   Phyllis: No, _____. I read a book instead.

9. (eat)   *Edward:* _____ you _____ anything at the party?

             Frank: No, _____. I _____ a sandwich before

                       the party.

10. (choose)   *George:* _____ you _____ the blue shirt?

             Harry: No, _____. I _____ the red shirt.

Part C Underline the correct word to complete each statement.

Example: Did you (<u>fall</u>, fell, felt) asleep early last night?

1. There was a lot of noise outside! Did you (here, hear, heard) it from your room?

2. Jason (sell, selled, sold) his boat for $10,000.

3. What time did you (leave, leaved, left) the party?

4. Did you (write, wrote, writed) a thank-you note to the hostess?

5. I didn't (understand, understanded, understood) the teacher, so I raised my hand.

6. Frank was in a lot of pain, so he (take, took, taked) some medicine.

7. I was very tired, so I (sleep, sleeped, slept) for several hours.

8. James was surprised when he (see, seed, saw) his girlfriend at the airport.

9. Karen has no money because she (lose, lost, losed) her purse.

10. I didn't want to wear a raincoat, so I (bring, bringed, brought) an umbrella.

TEST 12 Past Tense of Regular and Irregular Verbs

Clear Grammar 1, Unit 6

Name _____ Date _____

Part A Use the words to write statements and questions in the past tense. (If the sentence is negative [neg], write the negative form of the verb.)

1. Brian / (work) / in Paris / for a year _____.

2. Mary / (live [neg]) / in Italy / for a long time _____.

3. you / (study) / for yesterday's test _____?

4. the baby / (cry) / because she was hungry _____.

5. the audience / (like [neg]) / the movie _____.

6. you / (wash) / your clothes _____?

7. Dan and Sue / (go) / to Hawaii _____.

8. the parade / (stop) / on Fletcher Avenue _____.

9. the little boy / (run) / to his mother _____.

10. Sam / (write) / a letter / to his father _____.

Part B Read each sentence carefully. If the underlined part is correct, circle C. If the underlined part is wrong, circle X, and write the correct answer on the line. Six of the sentences are wrong.

C X 1. Jan and Marsha <u>did eat</u> a big breakfast yesterday morning.

_____

C X 2. Eric <u>ironed</u> his shirt before he went to work.

_____

C X 3. George coughed all night, so he <u>didn't slept</u> very well.

_____

C X 4. The hostess <u>introduced</u> her guests to each other at the party.

_____

C X 5. Although he was confused, Lee <u>no asked</u> any questions.

_____

C   X   6.   Harry <u>doesn't bought</u> enough soda for the picnic.

_____

C   X   7.   <u>You did forget</u> to set your alarm clock last night?

_____

C   X   8.   The doctor <u>gave</u> me a prescription for pain medication.

_____

C   X   9.   When I <u>heared</u> the phone ring, I ran inside.

_____

C   X   10.   <u>Did you speak</u> to your teacher about your homework?

_____

Part C   Underline the word or words that correctly complete each sentence.

1. The sun (begin, began) to set at 6:30 last night.

2. (Did you bring, Did you brought) your books home with you?

3. Brenda (visitted, visited) her friend in the hospital.

4. What time did you (left, leave) your house this morning?

5. Last night, I (putted, put) my cat outside before I (goed, went) to sleep.

6. The waiter (told, telled) us what the specials (was, were).

7. The teacher (thinked, thought) the students were prepared for the test.

8. (Did you wrote, Did you write) a grocery list?

9. It (snowed, snowwed) in New York last week.

10. (Was your teacher, Did your teacher) erase the blackboard?

TEST 13 *Wh-* Questions

Clear Grammar 1, Unit 7

Name _____   Date _____

Part A Fill in each blank with the correct question word: *who, what, when, where, which,* or *why.*

Example: Q: __When__ did you go to sleep?

A: I went to sleep at 10:00.

1. Q: __why__ did you study for a long time?

   A: Because I wanted to do well on the test.

2. Q: __who__ called you last night?

   A: Anthony called me last night.

3. Q: __which__ shoes did you decide to buy?

   A: I bought the black shoes.

4. Q: __what__ is the topic of your paper?

   A: popular tourist sites.

5. Q: __when__ were you born?

   A: I was born in Miami, Florida.

6. Q: __when__ did you get back from California?

   A: I got back on Thursday.

7. Q: __why__ were you absent from school yesterday?

   A: Because my car wouldn't start.

8. Q: __who__ gave you that sweater?

   A: My sister gave me this sweater.

9. Q: __where__ did you go on vacation?

   A: We went to Puerto Rico.

10. Q: __when__ were you born?

    A: I was born in 1966.

Part B Make a questions by substituting *who, why, what, when,* or *where* for the underlined words. Follow the example.

     Example: <u>Yolanda</u> cooked dinner.   *Who cooked dinner?*

1. Angela lives <u>in Texas</u>. *where does she live ?*
2. I went to Switzerland <u>in 1993</u>. *When did you go to Su... ?*
3. Uncle Charlie brought <u>CDs</u> to the party. *what did uncle brig to the park*
4. Jan works two jobs <u>because she needs money</u>. *why Does J work two job*
5. <u>Cheesecake</u> is my favorite dessert. *which is your favon dessert ..?*
6. Rosalie went <u>to the store</u>. *Where did Rosalie go ?*
7. <u>Olga</u> left a message for Jason. *Who left a message for jason*
8. I need to leave for the airport <u>at 5:00</u>. *When do you need to lea ...*
9. Don is nervous <u>because he's not ready for his test</u>. *Why is Don nervous -*
10. We studied <u>punctuation</u> in Grammar 101. *which do we study in gram 101*

Part C Circle the letter of the answer that correctly completes each sentence.

1. *Q:* "_____ that watch?"

   A: "At the mall."

   (A) When did you buy   (C) Where did you buy

   (B) Did you buy   (D) Where did you bought

2. *Q:* "_____ to the party?"

   A: "John did."

   (A) Who invited you   (C) Who did you invite

   (B) Who you invited   (D) Who invites you

3. *Q:* "_____ the football team?"

   A: "Because I don't have enough time to practice."

   (A) When did you quit   (C) Where did you quit

   (B) Why did you quit   (D) Who did you quit

4. *Q:* "_____ is the tallest building in the United States?"

   A: "I think it's the Sears Tower."

   (A) Who   (C) When

   (B) What   (D) Where

5. Q: "_____ did Nancy visit at the hospital?"

 A: "She visited her father."

 (A) Who   (C) Whom

 (B) Where ✓   (D) When

6. Q: "_____ can I get Ben & Jerry's ice cream?"

 A: "You can buy it at any store."

 (A) Where ✓   (C) When

 (B) Why   (D) Which

7. Q: "_____ is our next school holiday?"

 A: "I think it's July 4th."

 (A) Where   (C) Why

 (B) When ✓   (D) Who

8. Q: "_____ did you go to the party with?"

 A: "I went with Elena and Suzanne."

 (A) Who ✓   (C) Whom

 (B) Where   (D) Which

9. Q: "_____ for your birthday?"

 A: "I got two CDs and a DVD player."

 (A) Which did you get   (C) What got you

 (B) What you got   (D) What did you get ✓

10. Q: "_____ to graduate?"

 A: "In six months."

 (A) Why do you plan   (C) Why you plan

 (B) When do you plan ✓   (D) When you plan

TEST 14   *Wh-* Questions

Clear Grammar 1, Unit 7

Name _____   Date _____

Part A   Underline the word that correctly completes each sentence.

1. (Who, What, Where) do you live?

2. (What, When, Why) does this class begin?

3. (What, Which, Why) do you want to learn English?

4. (Who, Whom, What) bought your car for you?

5. (Whom, When, What) do you want for your birthday?

6. (When, Where, Which) university do you plan to attend?

7. (Which, When, Why) did you last talk to your family?

8. (Who, When, What) time do you usually go to sleep?

9. (Which, Why, When) didn't you do your homework last night?

10. (Where, When, Who) is your favorite actor?

Part B   Read each sentence and pay special attention to the underlined parts. If the underlined part is correct, circle C. If it is wrong, circle X, and write the correct answer on the line. Six of the sentences are wrong.

C   X   1.   When time does the airplane leave?
          what time

C   X   2.   Who student is your best friend?
          which

C   X   3.   Why did you spend so much money?
          _____

C   X   4.   Where is Greenland?
          _____

C   X   5.   What cooked dinner for you last night?   who
          _____

C   X   6.   What kinds of books do you like to read?
          _____

C   X   7. <u>Why</u> are my car keys?

when (handwritten)

_____

C   X   8. <u>When</u> do we need to be at the restaurant?

_____

C   X   9. <u>Where</u> does "curriculum" mean?

what (handwritten)

_____

C   X   10. <u>What</u> directed the movie *Titanic*?

who (handwritten)

_____

Part C Circle the letter of the answer that correctly completes each sentence.

1. *Q:* "_____ did you come to this country?"

  A: "In 2002."

  (A) Where   (C) When

  (B) What   (D) Who

2. *Q:* "_____ to school?"

  A: "In Florida."

  (A) Where do you go   (C) When do you go

  (B) What do you go   (D) Why do you go

3. *Q:* "_____ don't you like to swim?"

  A: "Because I'm afraid of the water."

  (A) Who   (C) What

  (B) Why   (D) Whom

4. *Q:* "_____ are the colors of the rainbow?"

  A: "They are red, orange, yellow, green, blue, purple, and violet."

  (A) Where   (C) When

  (B) What   (D) Why

5. *Q:* "_____ your favorite author?"

  A: "J.D. Salinger is my favorite author."

  (A) What is   (C) Why is

  (B) When is   (D) Who is

6. *Q:* "_____ do you like to travel with?"

   A: "I like to travel with my cousins."

   (A) Who   (C) Whom

   (B) Where   (D) When

7. *Q:* "_____ time does the football game start?"

   A: "It starts at 4:00."

   (A) When   (C) Where

   (B) What   (D) Why

8. *Q:* "_____ your job?"

   A: "I quit my job because I need to make more money."

   (A) When did you quit   (C) Where you quit

   (B) What you did quit   (D) Why did you quit

9. *Q:* "_____ want to meet for lunch?"

   A: "We can meet on Monday."

   (A) Where do you   (C) Why you do

   (B) When do you   (D) Who you

10. *Q:* "_____ taught you about religion?"

    A: "My parents did."

    (A) When   (C) Whom

    (B) Who   (D) Why

TEST 15 Word Order

Clear Grammar 1, Unit 8

Name _____   Date _____

Part A Write new sentences from the parts. Pay attention to the word order. Follow the example.

Example: live / in / I / in California / a large city   *I live in a large city in California.*

1. at 10:00 / I go to sleep / every night

   I go to sleep at 10:00 every night.

2. a house / Bill bought / in Texas

   Bill bought a house in Texas.

3. Harold drives / at 7:30 / to work

   Harold drives to work at 7:30.

4. a / car / red / Elaine wants

   Elaine wants a red car.

5. at 7:00 / at Lucy's house / The party is

   The party is at Lucy's house at 7:00

6. in a hotel / We stayed / in Zurich

   We stayed in a hotel in Zurich.

7. Kennedy was shot / on November 22 / at 12:30

   Kennedy was shot at 12:30 on November 22

8. Fred sailed / a / island / tropical / to

   Fred sailed to a tropical island

9. to school / for five hours / I go / every day

   I go to school for five hours every day

10. a / black / Brenda has / cat

    Brenda a black cat

Part B Circle the letter of the answer that correctly completes each sentence.

1. Justin will graduate _____.

   (A) month next from high school   (C) from high school next month

   (B) next high school from month   (D) next school from high month

2. Amber rented _____.

   (A) a house in a nice neighborhood   (C) in a nice neighborhood a house

   (B) a nice house in neighborhood   (D) in a nice house a neighborhood

3. Nina runs _____.

   (A) every day for minutes 30   (C) every day for 30 minutes

   (B) for 30 minutes every day   (D) every 30 minutes for days

4. Ann is from _____.

   (A) the Caribbean in a small island   (C) a small Caribbean in the island

   (B) an island small in the Caribbean   (D) a small island in the Caribbean

5. My plane leaves _____.

   (A) at 12:00 on Friday   (C) on Friday at 12:00

   (B) at Friday on 12:00   (D) on 12:00 at Friday

6. I keep all my pencils _____.

   (A) on my desk in a cup   (C) in a cup on my desk

   (B) on my cup in a desk   (D) in a desk on my cup

7. Keith and Kelly talked _____.

   (A) for 20 minutes last night   (C) for last night 20 minutes

   (B) for 20 nights last minute   (D) for the last minute

8. The _____ rushed into the house.

   (A) young boys   (C) boys young

   (B) youngs boys   (D) boys are young

9. Ben's mobile phone is _____.

   (A) in the garage in the car   (C) in the car in the garage

   (B) in the garage's car   (D) in the car's garage

10. I stayed _____.

    (A) for four hour at the library   (C) four for hours at the library

    (B) at the hours for four libraries   (D) at the library for four hours

Part C Underline the words that correctly complete each sentence. Follow the example.

Example: Suzanne bought a (car new, <u>new car</u>).

1. Elias has (brown hair, hair brown).

2. Becky's cat has (eyes green, green eyes).

3. We just took a (difficult test, test difficult)!

4. I hope you have a (happy birthday, birthday happy).

5. There was a (sunset beautiful, beautiful sunset) last night.

6. *Spiderman* was a (popular movie, movie popular).

7. Karen bought her (best friend, friend best) a (ring silver, silver ring) for her birthday.

8. Gail keeps her money in a (place secret, secret place) in her room.

9. Maria printed the party invitations on (yellow paper, paper yellow).

10. Thomas sailed a (boat 10-foot, 10-foot boat) across the (lake large, large lake).

Clear Grammar 1, Unit 8

Name _____ Date _____

Part A Write new sentences from the parts. Pay attention to the word order. Follow the example.

Example: in the afternoon / on the sofa / sleep / I *I sleep on the sofa in the afternoon.*

1. at 2:00 / in room 105 / have / We / a test

   We have a test in room 105 at 2:00.

2. was born / at 10 A.M. / My niece / on October 28th

   My niece was born at 10 A.m on October 28th.

3. at 6:00 / We're meeting / on Saturday / for dinner

   We're meeting for dinner at 6:00 on Saturday

4. Irene / roses / beautiful / got / from her boyfriend

   Irene got beautiful roses from her boyfriend

5. Linda / angry / is / now

   Linda is angry now

6. is / The concert / in St. Petersburg / on the 18th

   The concert is in St. Petersburg on the 18th.

7. bought / silver / car / a / Elaine

   Elaine bought a silver car

8. slept / in my room / by the chair / My cat

   My cat slept by the chair in my room

9. met / at the lake / at 9:00 / My friends

   My friends met at the lake at 9:00.

10. me / call / at noon / Please

    Call me at noon. pleas.

Part B Read each sentence and pay special attention to the underlined parts. If the underlined part is correct, circle C. If it is wrong, circle X, and write the correct answer on the line. Five of the sentences are wrong.

C   X   1. My mother cooked dinner <u>in the kitchen at 6:00</u>.

_____

C   X   2. I bought my sofa <u>in Ybor City at a furniture store</u>.

_____

C   X   3. We usually go to the beach <u>at 10 A.M. on Saturdays</u>.

_____

C   X   4. Miranda has a <u>cat black</u>.

_____

C   X   5. The library is <u>on Hillsborough Avenue in Tampa</u>.

_____

C   X   6. This <u>spaghetti is delicious</u>!

_____

C   X   7. Tom and Jerry ate a lot of <u>food fattening</u> on vacation.

_____

C   X   8. I loved the Guggenheim Museum when I went <u>last year there</u>.

_____

C   X   9. We went on a shopping spree <u>at the mall yesterday</u>.

_____

C   X   10. Mandy was <u>for two weeks in New York</u>.

_____

Part C Underline the word order that correctly completes each sentence.

1. Denise bought a (doll small, small doll) for her daughter.

2. Chris went (to a party at 10:00, at 10:00 to a party).

3. The plane arrives (at the airport at 7:45, at 7:45 at the airport).

4. Kim has a doctor's appointment (on Tuesday at noon, at noon on Tuesday).

5. Kathy found her car keys (in her room on a table, on a table in her room).

6. The moon will be full (at 1 A.M. on Friday, on Friday at 1 A.M.).

7. Lorie found some (puppies frightened, frightened puppies) under a tree near the lake.

8. There is some (water cold, cold water) in the refrigerator.

9. Irving celebrated his (birthday 70th, 70th birthday) two days ago.

10. Roxanne put her books (in her living room on a shelf, on a shelf in her living room).

TEST 17 Present Progressive Tense

Clear Grammar 1, Unit 9

Name _____   Date _____

Part A Fill in the blanks with the *present progressive form* of the verb in parentheses. Be careful! Some of the verbs can't be used in the present progressive tense. In that case, *use simple present tense instead*.

Example: Cindy (eat) ___is eating___ dinner right now.

1. Freddy (listen) ___is listening___ to music.
2. The children (study) ___are studying___ in their room.
3. David and Daniel (watch) ___are watching___ a football game.
4. Barry (like) ___likes___ to dance.
5. Stella (shop) ___is shopping___ at the mall.
6. I (need) ___need___ a new bicycle.
7. Our teacher (give) ___is giving___ us a test tomorrow.
8. Tony (run) ___is running___ right now.
9. Dawn (read) ___is reading___ a book.
10. I (love) ___love___ Fridays!

Part B Circle the letter of the answer that correctly completes each sentence.

1. Danny _____ in California this year.
   (A) is living   (C) lives
   (B) are living   (D) lived

2. Martha _____ a computer class this semester.
   (A) took   (C) takes
   (B) is takeing   (D) is taking

3. The shop _____ in 20 minutes.
   (A) is closing   (C) closed
   (B) closing   (D) close

4. It _____ outside, so we should take our jackets.
   (A) rains outside   (C) is raining
   (B) are raining   (D) raining

5. The children _____ a good time in the snow.

(A) having   (C) are having ✓

(B) is having   (D) are haveing

6. I can't go to work because _____ today.

(A) I am sick ✓   (C) I am being sick

(B) I sicking   (D) I am sicking

7. Sometimes _____ to lock my door.

(A) I'm forgetting   (C) I forgetting

(B) I forget ✓   (D) I'm forget

8. Louise _____ dinner in the kitchen.

(A) are cooking   (C) is cookeing

(B) cooking   (D) is cooking ✓

9. Paul _____ for the tennis tournament.

(A) is practicing ✓   (C) are practicing

(B) practicing   (D) is practiceing

10. _____ English, so I can follow news reports on T.V.

(A) I am understanding   (C) I understand ✓

(B) I understandeing   (D) I understanding

Part C Read each sentence. If it is correct, write C on the line. If it is wrong, write X on the line, and change the sentence to make it correct. Write the correction next to the sentence. Six sentences are not correct.

____✓ 1. The dog is eating food from a bowl. _____

____X 2. Linda <u>goes</u> to the mall tomorrow. *is going* _____

____X 3. The shark <u>is swiming</u> in the ocean. *m* _____

____X 4. Larry <u>is driveing</u> to Massachusetts for the winter holidays.

_____

____✓ 5. The teacher <u>is repeating</u> the instructions. _____

____X 6. Robby <u>is hiting</u> his brother. _____

____X 7. Steven <u>waiting</u> to find out what his grades are. _____

____✓ 8. My mother <u>is shouting</u> at me because she wants me to come inside.

_____

____✓ 9. The Miami Dolphins <u>are playing</u> a football game next weekend.

_____

____X 10. It looks like the porpoise <u>is smileing</u>. _____

TEST 18 Present Progressive Tense

Clear Grammar 1, Unit 9

Name _____   Date _____

Part A Fill in the blanks with the *present progressive form* of the verb in parentheses. If the verb cannot be used in the progressive, *use the simple present tense*. If the sentence is negative [neg], write the negative form of the verb. Follow the examples.

Examples: (study) Keiko ___*is studying*___ for her final exam.

(want) I ___*want*___ to have some ice cream.

1. Seong Min (practice) ___is practicing___ his pronunciation right now.
2. Our teacher (explain) ___is explaining___ the assignment to us.
3. Plants (need) ___need___ air and water to stay alive.
4. The astronaut (remember [neg]) ___didn't remember___ when the rocket launched.
5. Michelle (run) ___is running___ in a marathon next week.
6. Most people (prefer) ___prefer___ to stay inside on rainy days.
7. The event planner (count) ___is counting___ the number of chairs in the room.
8. Peggy (type) ___is typing___ a report to give to her boss.
9. If you (believe) ___believe___ in yourself, you can do anything.
10. The choir (sing) ___is singing___ a traditional song.
11. The children are in the living room, and they (watch) ___are watching___ television.
12. Rachel (love) ___loves___ her mother.
13. The cashier (talk) ___is talking___ to her boss to get approval for the credit charge.
14. This (be) ___is___ a perfect day!
15. Almost everyone (like) ___like___ dessert.

Part B Use the parts to make sentences and questions in the *present progressive tense*. If it is not possible to use the verb in the present progressive tense, *use the simple present tense*. Follow the example.

Example: (eat [neg]) / Dan / lunch / today ___*Dan is not eating lunch today.*___

1. (rain) / It / hard / right now ___It is raining right now___.

2. (dance) / Melissa and her husband ___M and her husband are dancing___

3. (go) / to the beach / this weekend / you ___Are you going to the beach___ ?

4. (understand) / the class / you / so far ___Are the class and you understand___

5. (know [neg]) / The little girl / how to wink ___The little girl doesnt know how___

6. (take) / a bath / right now / My mother ___My mother are taking a bath right___

7. (have) / a good time / in this country / you ___Are you having a good time in this cou___

8. (shop) / for a wedding dress / Marissa ___Ma............___

9. (own [neg]) / a car / Bob ___Bob___

10. (hear) / a bird / outside my window / I ___hear___

11. (begin) / to blow / The wind _____.

12. (write) / Stephen King / another book _____.

13. (close) / The store / in ten minutes _____.

14. (sit) / in her favorite chair / My grandmother _____.

15. (have) / two children / Paula _____.

TEST 19 Count vs. Noncount

Clear Grammar 1, Unit 10

Name _____   Date _____

Part A Fill in the blanks with *a, an, some,* or *any.*

1. I need to buy _____*a*_____ new notebook for class.

2. Carol doesn't have ____*any*____ paper, so she needs to buy some.

3. The elephant at the zoo ate _____*an*_____ apple and ____*some*____ peanuts.

4. Harvey doesn't have _____*any*_____ time to study because he has ____*a*____ job.

5. There is ___*an*___ amazing sale going on at the mall!

6. For breakfast, I had _____*some*_____ cereal and ____*a*____ piece of fruit.

7. After a day at the beach, I was surprised to find that there wasn't _____ sand in my shoes.

8. Monica waited for _____ hour to see the doctor.

9. Peggy made _____ reservation to fly to Hawaii for vacation.

10. We have _____ list of books we need to read for this class.

Part B Underline the quantity words that correctly complete each sentence.

1. The sky is dark, so we can't see (much, many) stars.

2. Richard gave his son (a few, a little) dollars to buy lunch.

3. There isn't (much, many) interest in disco music anymore.

4. I only have (a few, a little) money, so I can't buy expensive gifts.

5. Barbara put (some, any) oil in the pan before she baked her cake.

6. Amanda doesn't have (some, any) flour, so she can't make cookies.

7. This soup is terrible! There is too (much, many) salt in it.

8. Kathy is having trouble in class, so she asked her teacher for (a few, some) help.

9. The mechanic had (a few, a little) difficulty fixing the car.

10. Ellen was hungry, so she ate (a few, some) pizza.

Part C Look at the underlined part in the sentence. If the part is correct, write C in the blank. If the part is wrong, write X, and write the correct answer on the line. Five sentences are not correct.

_____ 1. Irene went to the store and bought <u>some</u> fish.

_____

_____ 2. There is <u>a</u> small bird in the tree outside.

_____

_____ 3. There isn't <u>some</u> sugar, so the coffee is bitter.

_____

_____ 4. The young bride had to make <u>many</u> choices before her wedding.

_____

_____ 5. After dinner, we decided to have <u>a few</u> pie.

_____

_____ 6. Patricia took <u>any</u> candy to school with her.

_____

_____ 7. We can't all have sandwiches because there isn't <u>much</u> bread.

_____

_____ 8. Rachel's <u>tooths</u> hurt, so she has to go to the dentist.

_____

_____ 9. Our teacher gave us <u>a</u> homework for tomorrow.

_____

___ 10. Do you want <u>any</u> cheese on your sandwich?

_____

TEST 20 Count vs. Noncount

Clear Grammar 1, Unit 10

Name _____   Date _____

Part A Circle the letter of the answer that correctly completes each sentence.

1. There is _____ water in the refrigerator if you're thirsty.

   (A) some   (C) a

   (B) any   (D) a few

2. Allan drank _____ glass of milk with his sandwich.

   (A) any   (C) a

   (B) some   (D) a few

3. The stereo has _____ CD player in it.

   (A) a few   (C) an

   (B) a   (D) much

4. The party is over, but there are still _____ people in the house.

   (A) a   (C) much

   (B) an   (D) some

5. Do you want _____ coffee with your dessert?

   (A) a   (C) some

   (B) many   (D) a few

6. After the party, we didn't have _____ ice left.

   (A) any   (C) some

   (B) an   (D) many

7. Kevin doesn't have _____ time, so he can only take short naps.

   (A) much   (C) many

   (B) a little   (D) some

8. There is _____ time left before the end of the semester.

   (A) a few   (C) many

   (B) any   (D) a lot of

9. My piano teacher took _____ minutes to help me with my chords.

   (A) a

   (C) any

   (B) a few

   (D) much

10. Martin cooked _____ hamburgers on the grill.

   (A) much

   (C) a

   (B) some

   (D) any

Part B Fill in the blanks with *there is* or *there are*.

1. _____ nine planets in the solar system.

2. _____ several reasons why college will benefit you.

3. _____ some bread baking in the oven.

4. _____ a few mushrooms left in the bowl.

5. _____ many grammar rules to learn.

6. _____ a lot of water in the tub.

7. _____ a little money in the bottom of my purse.

8. _____ some sheets of paper on the desk.

9. _____ a lot of sugar in this dessert.

10. _____ many challenges to face when you live in a foreign country.

Part C Underline the word that correctly completes each sentence.

1. We waited (an, a) hour for the doctor's office to open.

2. I don't need (some, any) help with these books.

3. The bakery has (many, much) kinds of pastries to choose from.

4. Joseph bought (a, some) furniture for his new apartment.

5. Norman caught (any, a) fish on his fishing trip.

6. Do you want (some, a) rice with your meal?

7. Mark took (any, some) time to think about his decision.

8. Jenny ate (a, some) piece of cake after dinner.

9. The teacher found (a, an) pencil under her desk.

10. Mike doesn't put (some, any) salt on his vegetables.

TEST 21 Prepositions

Clear Grammar 1, Unit 11

Name _____   Date _____

Part A Fill in the blanks with *in, on,* or *at.*

1. Phyllis was born _____ Seattle.

2. Our class starts _____ 9:00.

3. The parade will be _____ Main Street.

4. The new contract begins _____ January.

5. _____ Friday all of us are going to meet for lunch.

6. My aunt's birthday party will be _____ our house.

7. The Lincoln Memorial is _____ Washington, DC.

8. _____ 11:00 the restaurant begins serving lunch.

9. Michelle and I plan to spend this weekend _____ her cousin's place.

10. Are you available to meet for dinner _____ Monday?

Part B Circle the letter of the answer that correctly completes each sentence.

1. We ate breakfast _____.

   (A) at 8:00 in the morning   (C) at 8:00 the morning

   (B) at the morning   (D) in 8 o'clock

2. Diane works _____.

   (A) at the community college   (C) the community college

   (B) on the community college   (D) in the community college

3. Our family went to Maine _____ July 4th.

   (A) in   (C) at

   (B) on   (D) with

4. The first plane flight was _____.

   (A) in December 17   (C) on 1903

   (B) in 1903   (D) at December 17

5. We put a new table _____.

   (A) at our kitchen   (C) in our kitchen

   (B) our kitchen   (D) on our kitchen

6. Jo is _____.

   (A) at room 664   (C) in room 664

   (B) on room 664   (D) room 664

7. Tony goes to school _____ a public university _____ Los Angeles.

   (A) in . . . at   (C) in . . . on

   (B) on . . . in   (D) at . . . in

8. Darla ate dinner _____ an Italian restaurant _____ Green Street.

   (A) at . . . on   (C) at . . . in

   (B) in . . . on   (D) in . . . in

9. Sam likes to snow ski _____.

   (A) at the winter   (C) the winter

   (B) in the winter   (D) on the winter

10. The baseball game starts _____.

   (A) at noon   (C) on noon

   (B) in noon   (D) noon

Part C   Underline the word that correctly completes each sentence.

1. The teachers began their meeting (in, at) 9 A.M.

2. The young bride waited (on, in) her room for the wedding to begin.

3. The White House is (in, on) Pennsylvania Avenue (on, in) Washington, DC.

4. (At, On) 9 P.M. the fireworks display will begin.

5. Shannon met her boyfriend (in, at) McDonald's (on, in) Wilson Avenue.

6. Angie bought a house (in, on) Southwick Drive.

7. My plane landed (in, at) 10:00.

8. Jenny was surprised when the phone rang (at, in) 11:30 (at, in) night.

9. I was born (in, at) 7 A.M. (at, on) July 18.

10. Adam is (on, in) the hospital (at, on) Gallows Road.

TEST 22 Prepositions

Clear Grammar 1, Unit 11

Name _____   Date _____

Part A Write new sentences from the parts. Add the correct prepositions.

Example: live / I / Boston ___*I live in Boston.*___

1. eat / lunch / the cafeteria / We

   _____

2. go / to school / Fowler Avenue / I

   _____

3. met / our friends / Jake's Fine Italian Eatery / We

   _____

4. celebrated / the millennium / 2000 / The world

   _____

5. begins / The new year / midnight

   _____

6. ends / The weekend / Sunday

   _____

7. is / The Eiffel Tower / Paris

   _____

8. became / the President of the U.S. / 1789 / George Washington

   _____

9. have / a meeting / Monday / The managers

   _____

10. is / The college / Biscayne Boulevard

   _____

Part B Fill in the blanks with *in, on,* or *at.*

1. Abraham Lincoln was born _____ Springfield, Illinois.

2. The graduation ceremony was _____ the convention center.

3. The play starts _____ 7:30.

4. We're flying to Mexico _____ July 16th.

5. Amelia Earhart flew across the Atlantic _____ 1928.

6. I met my friends at our favorite restaurant _____ Siena Way.

7. Paula set her alarm clock to wake her up _____ 6 A.M.

8. Gregg saw a lot of his classmates _____ the library.

9. New Orleans is a city _____ Louisiana.

10. Henry Ford built his first car _____ 1896.

Part C Read each sentence carefully. If the sentence is correct, circle C. If the sentence is wrong, circle X, and write the correction on the line. Six of the sentences are wrong.

C   X   1.   Carol's workday ends at 5 P.M.

_____

C   X   2.   The first McDonald's was at California.

_____

C   X   3.   We have a shorter day of classes in Fridays.

_____

C   X   4.   The art show begins at 9:00.

_____

C   X   5.   The parade ends in 180th Street.

_____

C   X   6.   Florida has a lot of rain in July.

_____

C   X   7.   There was news of a robbery at a local store.

_____

C   X   8.   Barbara was born in February 2nd.

_____

C   X   9.   There are many cigar factories at Tampa.

_____

C   X   10.   The tourists took pictures at Washington, DC.

_____

Clear Grammar 1, Units 1–11

Name _____ Date _____

Part A Fill in the blanks with the correct form of the verb. Choose *simple present, present progressive,* or *simple past tense.*

1. In the 1960s, the Beatles (be) __was__ very popular.

2. Donna (cook) __cooks.__ dinner for her family every night.

3. I need to pick up the baby because she (cry) __is crying.__ .

4. When the teacher (open) __opend__ the door, we walked into the room.

5. Look! It (begin) __is beginning.__ to snow outside!

6. Jack (love) __loves.__ to eat chocolate cake. He eats a piece just about every day.

7. Did you (remember) _____ to call your mother?

8. J.R. (bring) _____ a sweater to the picnic last Saturday.

9. Marilyn and Harvey (go) _____ to the mall later today.

10. Eileen (read) _____ one book every week.

Part B Read the underlined part. If the part is correct, write C in the blank. If the part is wrong, write the correction next to it. Ten of the sentences are not correct.

_____ 1. Museum tours begin <u>at</u> 10 A.M. _____

_____ 2. There are <u>many</u> interesting places to visit in New York. _____

_____ 3. Barry <u>is loving</u> his baby sister. _____

_____ 4. Fred drives a <u>blue motorcycle</u>. _____

_____ 5. <u>Where did you went</u> to school when you were a child? _____

_____ 6. Kevin <u>stoped</u> at the store on his way home from work. _____

_____ 7. <u>You were</u> at home last night? _____

_____ 8. The little boy cried because he hurt <u>her</u> leg. _____

_____ 9. <u>Those</u> mountains in the distance are covered with snow. _____

_____ 10. Tracey <u>no likes</u> to exercise. _____

_____11. Do you think <u>him</u> is a good father? _____

_____12. I don't have <u>some</u> bread, so I have to go to the store. _____

_____13. There are <u>many flowers yellow</u> in the garden. _____

_____14. <u>Were you</u> in class at 9:00? _____

_____15. Nancy <u>goed</u> to Jamaica for vacation. _____

Part C Circle the letter of the answer that correctly completes each sentence.

1. Ben's sister is sad because _____ lost her pet parrot.

   (A) he   (C) I

   (B) she   (D) we

2. Ed _____ television every day.

   (A) watches   (C) does watch

   (B) watch   (D) does watches

3. "_____ shirt is pretty. Where did you buy it?"

   (A) This is   (C) These are

   (B) That   (D) Those

4. My roommate and I cleaned _____ apartment. It looks like a brand-new place!

   (A) him   (C) you

   (B) my   (D) our

5. Carl _____ in the army from 2000 until 2003.

   (A) is   (C) am

   (B) are   (D) was

6. Alita _____ her sister in California last month.

   (A) visits   (C) visited

   (B) visitted   (D) is visiting

7. _____ your office yesterday?

   (A) Where did you leave   (C) Where did you left

   (B) When did you leave   (D) When did you left

8. Our class meets _____.

    (A) in room 204 at 9:00   (C) at 204 room in 9:00

    (B) in 9:00 at room 204   (D) at 9:00 room 204

9. The doctor _____ to check on her patient right now.

    (A) comes   (C) is comeing

    (B) coming   (D) is coming

10. If you have _____ time, I need to talk to you.

    (A) many   (C) a little

    (B) a lot   (D) a few

Part D Underline the word that correctly completes each sentence.

1. Barry and Carol met (on, at) the Chinese restaurant (in, on) Fletcher Avenue.

2. I bought (an, any) umbrella at the mall.

3. Melinda (is smileing, is smiling) because her friends bought her a cake.

4. Tom Cruise is (a handsome man, a man handsome).

5. (When you are going, When are you going) to Texas?

6. Kim (studied, studyed) for three hours last night.

7. Hal doesn't work, so he (is, was) home every day.

8. (Were the pilots, The pilots were) ready for the flight?

9. Tony ironed (his, him) pants because they were wrinkled.

10. (This, These) pizza is delicious!

11. (Does play Jason, Does Jason play) baseball?

12. (Does your father, Do your father) (speaks, speak) English?

13. New Year's Day is celebrated (on, in) January.

14. I (want, am wanting) a hot fudge sundae.

15. Why (you quit, did you quit) smoking?

TEST 24 Review of Book 1

Clear Grammar 1, Units 1–11

Name _____   Date _____

Part A Read each sentence carefully. If the sentence is correct, circle C. If the sentence is wrong, circle X, and write the correction on the line. Eight of the sentences are wrong.

C   X   1. Michael knows how to solve difficult problems.

_____

C   X   2. Are people waiting in line to buy movie tickets?

_____

C   X   3. When games are you going to play at the carnival?

_____

C   X   4. Those cats following their mother.

_____

C   X   5. Danny lives at a small house.

_____

C   X   6. I bought some tomatoes at the produce stand.

_____

C   X   7. Oliver went to sleep at 10:00.

_____

C   X   8. You did invite all of your friends to the party?

_____

C   X   9. The managers wasn't at the monthly meeting.

_____

C   X   10. Allison no listens to music in her car.

_____

C   X   11. I am not liking this spaghetti.

_____

C   X   12. Why did you come to work late this morning?

_____

C   X   13.   You don't need many time to exercise if you do it correctly.

_____

C   X   14.   The newly married couple spent a week in Martinique.

_____

C   X   15.   Were you in your country last year?

_____

Part B   Write new questions from the parts. Pay attention to the tense you need to use.

1. understand / the lesson / you [simple present]

_____

2. try / to learn English / your mother [present progressive]

_____

3. put / salt on your food / you / why [simple present]

_____

4. buy / a / shirt / blue / you [simple past]

_____

5. have / any / money / you [simple present]

_____

6. go / to the beach / on Saturday / you [present progressive]

_____

7. be / good student / a / you / when you were a child [simple past]

_____

8. see / you / the sunset [simple past]

_____

9. know / how many / people / in the U.S. / you [simple present]

_____

10. enjoy / your time / in this country / you [present progressive]

_____

Part C Underline the word that correctly completes each sentence.

1. *Q:* "Does your mother know how to sew?"

   A: "Yes, (she does, she is)."

2. I have (few, many) clean shirts, so I need to do my laundry.

3. Thomas and his wife (are, is) in Maryland right now.

4. *Q:* "Is (that, those) a good book?"

   A: "Yes, it is."

5. I found a (bird green, green bird) in my backyard.

6. When I was sick, I spent a lot of time (in, on) my room.

7. New Year's Day is (in, on) January 1st (on, in) the United States.

8. There (weren't, wasn't) any trains at the station when we arrived.

9. Walter (didn't like, didn't liked) the new brand of soda he (buy, bought).

10. *Q:* "(Where, When) are you going on vacation?"

    A: "I'm going to Las Vegas."

11. Frances (loves, is loving) her children.

12. (These, This) tea is too hot!

13. We don't have (some, any) time to prepare for the test.

14. There are (a lot of, much) movies available at the video store.

15. *Q:* "(Are you liking, Do you like) to dance?"

    A: "Yes."

Part D Circle the letter of the answer that correctly completes each sentence.

1. The boss _____ to work today.

   (A) no is coming   (C) isn't coming

   (B) not coming   (D) isn't comeing

2. My grandmother _____ in Kentucky.

   (A) is liveing   (C) living

   (B) is lives   (D) lives

3. _____ to get to school so early?

   (A) Why you want   (C) Why are you want

   (B) Why do you want   (D) Why want you

4. _____ is a challenging problem!

   (A) Thats   (C) This

   (B) These   (D) Those

5. "Hurry up! We only have _____ minutes before we need to catch our bus."

   (A) many   (C) a little

   (B) any   (D) a few

6. Elvis Presley was born _____.

   (A) on Tennessee   (C) at Tennessee

   (B) Tennessee   (D) in Tennessee

7. The baby _____ sick, so her parents _____ her to the doctor.

   (A) was . . . taking   (C) was . . . took

   (B) is . . . taking   (D) is . . . were takeing

8. _____ the restaurant to make a reservation?

   (A) You call   (C) Were you call

   (B) You called   (D) Did you call

9. _____ arrive in San Diego?

   (A) When does the boat   (C) What does the boat

   (B) When time does the boat (D) The boat

10. _____ when he opened his presents?

   (A) Were your boyfriend happy   (C) Was your boyfriend happy

   (B) Does your boyfriend happy   (D) Your boyfriend was happy

TEST 25 Articles

Clear Grammar 2, Unit 2

Name _____ Date _____

Part A Fill in the blanks with one of these: *a, an, the, ø* (for no article).

1. I bought _____ shirt today. _____ shirt is red.

2. Did you see _____ black cat outside in the garden?

3. _____ good student is one who studies a lot.

4. This is _____ uncomfortable chair!

5. Barbara needs _____ sugar for her cake recipe.

6. _____ United States includes several time zones.

7. The train is leaving in _____ hour.

8. These potatoes need _____ salt.

9. George W. Bush is _____ President of the United States.

10. I have _____ terrible headache.

Part B Look at the underlined part in the following sentences. If the part is correct, write C in the blank. If it is wrong, write the answer next to the sentence. Five of the sentences are not correct.

_____ 1. <u>The black car</u> is my favorite._____

_____ 2. Did you get <u>a new watch</u>?_____

_____ 3. Jerry bought a new suit. <u>The suit</u> is dark blue. _____

_____ 4. Elena told me she read <u>the interesting book</u> last week. _____

_____ 5. <u>The Nile River</u> is the longest river in the world._____

_____ 6. <u>The gold</u> is an expensive metal. _____

_____ 7. Where did you put <u>a remote control</u>?_____

_____ 8. The earth revolves around <u>a sun</u>. _____

_____ 9. I went to the beach, and now I have <u>a sand</u> in my hair. _____

___ 10. Sharon has a big house. <u>The house</u> has five rooms._____

Part C Circle the letter of the answer that correctly completes each sentence.

1. Elizabeth is _____ of Great Britain.

   (A) a queen   (C) an queen

   (B) the queen   (D) a queens

2. Maria speaks _____ very well.

   (A) English   (C) a English

   (B) an English   (D) the English

3. Elias likes to watch _____ on television.

   (A) the hockey   (C) a hockey

   (B) an hockey   (D) hockey

4. I don't like _____ in this restaurant.

   (A) a way they cook pasta   (C) the way they cook pasta

   (B) an way they cook pasta   (D) way they cook pasta

5. Arlene ate _____ for a snack.

   (A) apple   (C) a apple

   (B) an apple   (D) apple an

6. Henry has _____ big television. _____ screen is 54 inches wide.

   (A) the . . . A   (C) a . . . An

   (B) a . . . The   (D) an . . . A

7. _____ are very slow animals.

   (A) A turtles   (C) Turtles

   (B) The turtles   (D) An turtles

8. _____ was _____ first president of the United States.

   (A) George Washington . . . a   (C) The George Washington . . . the

   (B) George Washington . . . an   (D) George Washington . . . the

9. I went to _____ Jeanie's house.

   (A) a   (C) an

   (B) the   (D) ø

10. My sister and I have _____ same last name.

    (A) a   (C) an

    (B) the   (D) ø

TEST 26 Articles

Clear Grammar 2, Unit 2

Name _____ Date _____

Part A Fill in the blanks with one of these: *a, an, the, ø* (for no article).

1. We saw _____ orangutan at the zoo last week.

2. Our professor gave a lecture about _____ history of _____ Aztec Indians.

3. There was _____ old, ugly dog on _____ steps of my apartment.

4. _____ bananas have a lot of carbohydrates.

5. Many people think Mel Gibson is _____ handsome.

6. Cindy sat in _____ kitchen and waited for _____ spaghetti to boil.

7. At first, people didn't believe that _____ earth is round.

8. Usually, I like _____ cake, but I don't like _____ cake at this restaurant.

9. Tony Blair returned to _____ Great Britain after his trip to _____ Netherlands.

10. Joe's Restaurant makes _____ best crabs I have ever eaten!

Part B Underline the article that correctly completes each sentence.

1. When you make (a, an) pie, you should wait (a, an) hour before you cut it.

2. There is (a, an) unique movie theater in downtown Chicago.

3. (The, A) students in our vocabulary class are (the, ø) intelligent.

4. Teddy found (an, ø) old watch in (a, the) sand at (an, the) beach.

5. Lorraine made (a, the) sandwich, and then she ate (a, the) sandwich with some chips.

6. Olga stopped at (ø, the) bank on her way home from (a, the) office.

7. (A, The) beach is (a, the) worst place to visit when it's raining.

8. I went to (ø, the) doctor because (the, my) stomach hurts.

9. Greg Louganis won (a, an) gold medal in diving at (ø, the) Olympics.

10. Alberto wants to speak (the, ø) English so he can get a good job in his country.

Clear Grammar 2

TEST 27   *Be Going To* + VERBS

Clear Grammar 2, Unit 3

Name _____   Date _____

Part A Write a new sentence using the future form of the verb. Follow the example.

EVERY DAY	TOMORROW
Example: I brush my teeth.	*I am going to brush my teeth.*
1. I eat eggs for breakfast.	_____
2. I go to sleep at 10 P.M.	_____
3. I watch the news.	_____

NOW	TOMORROW
4. I am reading a book.	_____
5. Brad is resting.	_____
6. Yolanda is studying.	_____

YESTERDAY	TOMORROW
7. Charlie practiced pronunciation.	_____
8. David bought a newspaper.	_____
9. I ran three miles.	_____
10. Evan took a test.	_____

Part B Read the underlined parts. If the part is correct, write C in the blank. If it is wrong, write the correct answer on the line. Five sentences are not correct.

_____ 1. I <u>am not going to leave</u> Virginia today.

_____

_____ 2. <u>Are you going call</u> your mother tonight?

_____

_____ 3. <u>Is Don going to go</u> to the post office?

_____

_____ 4. Felix <u>going to register</u> for classes tomorrow.

_____

_____ 5. Harold <u>isn't going to ask</u> his boss for a raise in salary.

_____

_____ 6. <u>Nancy's is going to buy</u> presents for her children.

_____

_____ 7. <u>Gene is going to cooks</u> Thanksgiving dinner.

_____

_____ 8. <u>Are your parents going to pay</u> for your education?

_____

_____ 9. I <u>am going to order</u> some pizza.

_____

_____ 10. <u>Irene going to graduate</u> in June.

_____

Part C Underline the form of the verb that correctly completes each sentence.

1. Joanie (is going to leave, leaves, left) her house in ten minutes.

2. I (am going to visit, visit, visited) my sister next month.

3. Last week Kathy (went, goes, is going to go) to Florida.

4. It (is going to snow, is snowing, snows) right now.

5. Nancy (is going to be, is, is being) happy these days.

6. Lee and Marvin (call, called, are calling) their grandfather yesterday.

7. I (am going to write, write, wrote) my research paper last weekend.

8. The concert (is going to begin, begin, began) in an hour.

9. Norman (is going to sail, sailed, sails) his boat next Saturday.

10. Michael (is going to play, is playing, plays) the piano right now.

TEST 28 *Be Going To* + VERBS

Clear Grammar 2, Unit 3

Name _____   Date _____

Part A Circle the letter of the answer that correctly completes each sentence.

1. _____ to Naples for vacation next month.

   (A) We not going to go   (C) We aren't go

   (B) We're not to go   (D) We are not going to go

2. _____ on Saturday?

   (A) Is it rainning   (C) Is it going to rain

   (B) It is going to rain   (D) Is going to rain

3. _____ hard last night?

   (A) Are you study   (C) Did you study

   (B) You study   (D) Are you going to study

4. _____ busy this weekend, so I won't be able to come to your house.

   (A) I'm going to   (C) I'm going to be

   (B) I am being   (D) I was

5. Patty always _____ her teeth after every meal.

   (A) brushes   (C) is going to be brushing

   (B) going to brush   (D) is being brushed

6. _____ you any time soon?

   (A) Your parents are going to visit   (C) Are your parents going to visit

   (B) Are your parents visited   (D) Your parents visiting

7. Norma _____ her children with their homework later tonight.

   (A) helps   (C) is helped

   (B) is going to help   (D) is going help

8. Bob and Cheryl _____ a pool party next Sunday.

   (A) are having   (C) going to have

   (B) had   (D) have

9. John needs to lose some weight, so _____ 30 minutes a day next week.

   (A) walks   (C) he walked

   (B) he walking   (D) he is going to walk

10. Wilma _____ to the radio right now.

    (A) is not listening   (C) listens not

    (B) didn't listened   (D) not going to listen

11. Bart _____ eggs for breakfast.

    (A) is going to make   (C) going to make

    (B) is makeing   (D) is going to making

12. _____ full tomorrow night?

    (A) Was the moon   (C) Is the moon going to be

    (B) Is the moon being   (D) The moon is going to be

13. _____ difficult?

    (A) Is tomorrow's test going to be   (C) Tomorrow's test is going to be

    (B) Was tomorrow's test   (D) Tomorrow's test was

14. _____ for the competition?

    (A) Did the athletes going to practice   (C) Are the athletes practiceing

    (B) Are the athletes going to practice   (D) Do the athletes going to practice

15. The neighborhood pool _____ open during the winter.

    (A) isn't going to be   (C) no is going to be

    (B) isn't being   (D) no is to be

Part B Fill in the blanks with the correct form of the verb in parentheses, paying attention to the time clues.

1. (read)   Marshall _____ a book right now.

2. (need)   I know I _____ more sugar when I start baking later.

3. (play)   Carol _____ the piano for several hours last night.

4. (call)   Julia _____ her father every week.

5. (buy)   Evan _____ his first car earlier this morning.

6. (do)   Philip _____ his homework later tonight before he goes
            to bed.

7. (send)   Danny _____ a letter to his sister two days ago.

8. (like)   Sally _____ to sleep late on weekends.

9. (know)   Anna _____ how to play the guitar.

10. (try)   George _____ to visit all of his friends when he is
          in Ohio next month.

TEST 29 Irregular Past Tense

Clear Grammar 2, Unit 4

Name _____ Date _____

Part A Underline the word or words that correctly complete each sentence.

1. Oscar (leaves, left) his office at 5:00 every day.

2. I didn't (know, knew) where to go on the first day of class.

3. Marsha (keeps, kept) the letter from her boyfriend until 1997.

4. (Did you go, Did you went) to the circus last weekend?

5. Peter (didn't felt, didn't feel) well, so he (go, went) home.

6. (What did you do, What you did) when you (see, saw) the accident?

7. When (did it begin, did it began) to rain?

8. The old man (fall, fell) and (break, broke) his leg.

9. Richard (didn't bring, didn't brought) anything to eat for lunch.

10. The little girl (maked, made) a birthday card for her father.

Part B Answer these questions with complete sentences. Follow the example.

Example: Did Stan buy you a present? (yes)

_____*Yes, he bought me a purse.*_____

1. Did Tom give you any money? (no)

   _____

2. Did you wear a hat today? (yes)

   _____

3. Did you tell your mother about your grades? (no)

   _____

4. Did the teacher take your homework? (yes)

   _____

5. Did William swim in the pool with you? (no)

   _____

6. Did you meet new people at the party? (yes)

_____

7. Did you speak to your teacher? (no)

_____

8. Did Vivian say hello when she saw you? (yes)

_____

9. Did Albert send you a postcard? (no)

_____

10. Did you think about my suggestion? (yes)

_____

Part C Circle the letter of the answer that correctly completes each sentence.

1. I _____ to the doctor because I _____ sick.

   (A) went . . . going   (C) went . . . was

   (B) go . . . went   (D) going . . . went

2. _____ well?

   (A) Did you slept   (C) Did you sleeped

   (B) Did you sleep   (D) You did slept

3. Carol _____ a card to her sister on her birthday.

   (A) didn't send   (C) send

   (B) didn't sent   (D) didn't sends

4. _____ what the teacher said?

   (A) You understood   (C) Did you understood

   (B) Did you understand   (D) Do you understood

5. Rachel _____ out the candles on her birthday cake.

   (A) blow   (C) did blows

   (B) blew   (D) did blow

6. _____ that noise? I don't know what it was.

   (A) Did you heard   (C) You heard

   (B) Do you heard   (D) Did you hear

7. The flower I planted _____ at all.

   (A) didn't grew   (C) no grew

   (B) didn't growed   (D) didn't grow

8. _____ your house key?

   (A) Do you found   (C) Did you find

   (B) Do you find   (D) You did find

9. I _____ three glasses of water after the race.

   (A) drink   (C) drank

   (B) drinks   (D) drinked

10. The workers _____ the library next to the gas station.

    (A) build   (C) builds

    (B) builded   (D) built

101 Clear Grammar Tests **TEST 29**

Clear Grammar 2

TEST 30 Irregular Past Tense

Clear Grammar 2, Unit 4

Name _____   Date _____

Part A Read each sentence carefully, and pay special attention to the underlined part. If the underlined part is correct, circle C. If it is wrong, circle X, and write the correct answer on the line. Five of the sentences are wrong.

C   X   1.   George W. Bush <u>became</u> President in January of 2001.

_____

C   X   2.   After the bad dog <u>bited</u> me, I needed to go to the doctor.

_____

C   X   3.   Angela <u>didn't had</u> a pencil, so Kim lent her one.

_____

C   X   4.   <u>Did you knew</u> that people are weightless in space?

_____

C   X   5.   Six of the children <u>hid</u>, and the seventh child had to find them.

_____

C   X   6.   Henry was short for a long time, and then he <u>grew</u> six inches.

_____

C   X   7.   Laura <u>gived</u> her husband a leather jacket for his birthday.

_____

C   X   8.   Theresa <u>had</u> trouble learning grammar.

_____

C   X   9.   Our family <u>eated</u> a big dinner last Sunday.

_____

C   X   10.   I was so tired from working that I <u>did</u> nothing all weekend.

_____

Part B Write new sentences and questions from the parts. Be sure to use the correct form of the past tense verb.

1. (lead) / across the street / her babies / The mother duck

   The mother duck led her babies across the street.

2. (break) / my cell phone / I

   _____.

3. (forget) / to buy milk / you

   _____?

4. (draw) / a picture / The artist / with black ink

   _____.

5. (buy) / painting supplies / you / for your project

   _____?

6. (find) / an old photo album / I / in my closet

   _____.

7. (drink) / hot tea / because she was sick / Emily

   _____.

8. (cost) / a lot of money / your car

   _____?

9. (swim) / for two hours / Jill

   _____.

10. (put) / the dishes / in the sink / you

    _____?

Part C Fill in the blank with the correct past tense form of the verb in parentheses.

1. (take)   We _____ our first vocabulary test this morning.

2. (let)   Did you _____ your daughter help you bake the cake?

3. (win)   Pete Sampras _____ the tennis match.

4. (say)   The judge _____ the prisoner was guilty.

5. (build)   Oscar _____ a dog house for his dog.

6. (lose)   Jerry is upset because he _____ the ring his father gave him.

7. (mean)   What did you _____ by "interesting"?

8. (fall)   Did you hurt yourself when you _____ out of the tree?

9. (run)   Yolanda _____ in a 5K race.

10. (choose) Why did you _____ to come to this particular university?

TEST 31 *How* Questions

Clear Grammar 2, Unit 5

Name _____   Date _____

Part A Underline the correct words to complete each question.

1. *Q:* How (often, old, long) is your son?

    A: He's ten.

2. *Q:* How (tall, much, many) children do you have?

    A: I have three children.

3. *Q:* How (long, far, often) do you exercise?

    A: Five days a week.

4. *Q:* How (far, much, many) cake do you want?

    A: I want a lot!

5. *Q:* How (much, tall, far) is this ceiling?

    A: Twelve feet.

6. *Q:* How (much, many, old) rooms do you have in your house?

    A: Three.

7. *Q:* How (tired, tall, sad) are you?

    A: I feel like I could fall asleep right now.

8. *Q:* How (many, much, tall) do you weigh?

    A: 120 pounds.

9. *Q:* How (many, much, often) do you call your parents?

    A: Once a week.

10. *Q:* How (old, tired, angry) was your father about the broken window?

    A: He was very mad! He yelled for an hour!

Part B Fill in the blanks with the correct question words.

1. Q: _How old_ is your car?

    A: I bought it three years ago, so it's three years old.

2. Q: _How long_ were you in France?

    A: For two weeks.

3. Q: _How tall_ are you?

    A: I'm five feet tall.

4. Q: _How far_ is Tampa from Miami?

    A: It's 260 miles away.

5. Q: _____ is this semester?

    A: It's 16 weeks long.

6. Q: _How long_ time do you have?

    A: I don't have a lot of time. I only have five minutes.

7. Q: _How many_ people did you invite to the party?

    A: I invited 20 people.

8. Q: _How much_ did that sandwich cost?

    A: It cost $4.

9. Q: _How long_ do you plan to be here?

    A: I plan to be here for six months.

10. Q: _How old_ is your dog?

    A: He's six years old.

Part C Write a *how* question for these sentences. The underlined words can help you write the correct question.

1. T.J. is <u>six feet</u> tall.

   _____

2. Florida is <u>3,000 miles</u> away from California.

   _____

3. My father is <u>82 years old</u>.

   _____

4. I have <u>$5</u> in my wallet.

   _____

5. There are <u>six</u> puppies in the backyard.

   _____

6. There were <u>30</u> people at the party.

   _____

7. I wash clothes <u>twice a week</u>.

   _____

8. This class is <u>an hour long</u>.

   _____

9. My house is <u>1,500 square feet</u>.

   _____

10. My grandmother was <u>84 years old</u> when she died.

   _____

Clear Grammar 2

Clear Grammar 2, Unit 5

Name _____   Date _____

Part A Circle the letter of the answer that correctly completes each sentence.

1. How _____ eggs are in a dozen?

   (A) many   (C) much

   (B) often   (D) some

2. How _____ sugar does the recipe require?

   (A) many   (C) much

   (B) long   (D) often

3. _____ vacuum the carpet?

   (A) How many do you   (C) How often you do

   (B) How often do you   (D) Often how do you

4. _____ was the final exam?

   (A) What difficult   (C) How difficult

   (B) Why difficult   (D) Who difficult

5. How _____ is your school from your house?

   (A) long   (C) much

   (B) many   (D) far

6. How _____ is the airplane flight?

   (A) far   (C) often

   (B) long   (D) many

7. How _____ in your family?

   (A) much people are there   (C) many people are there

   (B) tall people are there   (D) many person are there

8. How _____ do we have to solve these problems?

   (A) many time   (C) time much

   (B) much time   (D) time many

9. How _____ in your city?

   (A) often it does rain

   (B) much does rain

   (C) many does it rains

   (D) often does it rain

10. How _____?

    (A) tall you are

    (B) are you tall

    (C) you are tall

    (D) tall are you

11. How _____ in your country?

    (A) expensive are the schools

    (B) are the schools expensive

    (C) the schools are expensive

    (D) are expensive the schools

12. How _____?

    (A) old your youngest child is

    (B) your youngest child is old

    (C) old is your youngest child

    (D) much child is your youngest

13. How _____ in your house?

    (A) are there many rooms

    (B) many rooms are there

    (C) are many rooms there

    (D) many are rooms there

14. How _____ for those shoes?

    (A) many did you pay

    (B) many you paid

    (C) much you paid

    (D) much did you pay

15. How _____ when you saw your parents?

    (A) happy were you

    (B) happy did you

    (C) you were happy

    (D) much were you

Part B Read each question carefully, and pay special attention to the underlined part. If the underlined part is correct, circle C. If it is wrong, circle X, and write the correction on the line. Six of the questions are wrong.

C X 1. Q: "<u>How much</u> brothers and sisters do you have?"

A: "I have one brother and one sister."

_____

C X 2. Q: "<u>How much</u> bread do we have in the house?"

A: "Not a lot. We need to buy some."

_____

C X 3. Q: "<u>How many</u> does your teacher give you homework?"

A: "Almost every night."

_____

C X 4. Q: "<u>What spicy</u> is your food?"

A: "It is very spicy."

_____

C X 5. Q: "<u>How tall</u> is your hair?"

A: "It's just past my shoulders."

_____

C X 6. Q: "<u>How many</u> stars are there in the sky?"

A: "I have no idea. I could never count them all."

_____

C X 7. Q: "<u>How much</u> ago did you come to this country?"

A: "I came here five months ago."

_____

C X 8. Q: "<u>What big</u> is your hometown?"

A: "It's very small."

_____

C X 9. Q: "<u>How long</u> is the movie?"

A: "It's about two hours long."

_____

C X 10. Q: "<u>How tired</u> are you?"

A: "I am very tired! I need to go to sleep!"

_____

Clear Grammar 2

TEST 33 Adverbs of Frequency

Clear Grammar 2, Unit 6

Name _____   Date _____

Part A Underline the word or words that correctly complete each sentence.

1. Alfred (is always, always is) late.

2. Candace (never eats, eats never) vegetables.

3. Ernest (is seldom, seldom is) awake at midnight.

4. The teacher (gives usually, usually gives) us homework over the weekend.

5. Gloria (rarely is, is rarely) hungry before noon.

6. I (am sometimes, sometimes am) too tired to wake up in the morning.

7. Jack (asks often, often asks) questions in class.

8. Yvonne (isn't never, is never) in class on time.

9. Don (usually studies, studies usually) before school.

10. Nancy (always is, is always) happy to see her children.

Part B Circle the letter of the answer that correctly completes each sentence.

1. *Q:* "Do you _____ skip breakfast?"

   A: "No, never."

   (A) never   (C) ever

   (B) how often   (D) not never

2. Lucille _____ tea in the morning.

   (A) drinks always   (C) always drinks

   (B) drinks rarely   (D) ever drinks

3. On Fridays, we _____ a video.

   (A) usually rent   (C) rent usually

   (B) are usually rent   (D) usually are rent

4. *Q:* "Do you _____ to museums?"

   A: "Yes, often."

   (A) go ever   (C) ever go

   (B) never go   (D) never goes

5. Melissa almost never goes to the beach. She _____ time.

(A) seldom have

(C) usually have

(B) usually has

(D) seldom has

6. *Q:* "How often do you read the newspaper?"

   A: "I _____ the time to read it."

(A) have rarely

(C) ever have

(B) rarely have

(D) have ever

7. *Q:* "_____ travel?"

   A: "No. I have no money, so I never travel."

(A) Do you never

(C) You do never

(B) Do you ever

(D) Ever do you

8. Nicky watches television most of the time. He _____ watches television.

(A) sometimes

(C) ever

(B) never

(D) usually

9. Tyler almost never studies. He _____ because he doesn't have time.

(A) often studies

(C) studies often

(B) rarely studies

(D) studies rarely

10. Kenny is at home much of the time. He _____ because he likes privacy.

(A) is often home

(C) often is home

(B) is seldom home

(D) is home seldom

Part C Write a new sentence using a frequency word in place of the underlined words.

1. The nurses are polite <u>all of the time</u>. _____

2. Debbie does <u>not</u> play piano <u>at any time</u>. _____

3. Kimberly is happy <u>most of the time</u>. _____

4. Marshall <u>almost never</u> goes to the theater. _____

5. My cat sleeps on the floor <u>most of the time</u>. _____

6. The infant is hungry <u>much of the time</u>. _____

7. Nancy <u>almost never</u> sleeps for eight hours. _____

8. We have tests <u>some of the time</u>. _____

9. Tony and Nina do <u>not</u> argue <u>at any time</u>. _____

10. This room is cold <u>much of the time</u>. _____

Clear Grammar 2, Unit 6

Name _____   Date _____

Part A Read each sentence carefully. If the sentence is correct, circle C. If it is wrong, circle X, and write the correction on the line. Five of the sentences are wrong.

C   X   1.   Charles <u>always helps</u> his father work on the car.

_____

C   X   2.   Vicki and her husband <u>never are</u> far from their children.

_____

C   X   3.   <u>Do you ever forget</u> to turn off the oven?

_____

C   X   4.   People who live in Louisiana <u>usually like</u> spicy food.

_____

C   X   5.   Students <u>score seldom</u> 100% on major exams.

_____

C   X   6.   I <u>often am</u> in bed by 10:00.

_____

C   X   7.   <u>Do you ever fall asleep</u> with the television on?

_____

C   X   8.   Fish <u>like never</u> to be out of water.

_____

C   X   9.   The sun <u>isn't never</u> in the sky at night.

_____

C   X   10.   Peter <u>sometimes puts</u> cream in his coffee.

_____

Part B Write a new sentence using a frequency word in place of the words in parentheses. Be careful where you put the frequency word!

1. Francesca is in Italy (some of the time).

   _____

2. I have grapefruit for breakfast (most of the time).

   _____

3. Our father cooks dinner (not at any time).

   _____

4. Our teacher comes to class early (all of the time).

   _____

5. My cat sleeps in my bed (almost never).

   _____

6. Jared and his best friend talk on the phone (much of the time).

   _____

7. The sky is dark when I wake up (all of the time).

   _____

8. The salespeople are helpful (some of the time).

   _____

9. Our grandmother is happy to see us (all of the time).

   _____

10. My friends like to dance (none of the time).

   _____

Part C Write new sentences from the parts. Pay special attention to where you put the frequency word.

1. always / Richard / rides / his bike / to school

   _____

2. never / cheats / on tests / Joanna

   _____

3. usually / clear / The sky / is / during the summer

   _____

4. rarely / visit / me / My neighbors

   _____

5. often / stressed / are / Doctors

   _____

6. always / Fred / calls / his brother / on his birthday

   _____

7. never / learn / a new language / immediately / People

   _____

8. often / have health problems / Older people

   _____

9. usually / am / in a bad mood / I / on Mondays

   _____

10. rarely / like / to take baths / Dogs

    _____

TEST 35 Object Pronouns

Clear Grammar 2, Unit 7

Name _____   Date _____

Part A Fill in the blanks with *me, you, him, her, it, us,* or *them.*

1. I am going to the library. Do you want to come with __me__?

2. There are two birds in the tree outside. Can you see __it__?

3. If you need help with your homework, I can help __you__.

4. Elena and I are going to go to the mall. Do you want to come with __them__?

5. Bob just left. Did you see __him__ as you came in?

6. The Eiffel Tower is supposed to be beautiful. I really want to see _____.

7. I can't find Lisa. When did you last see _____?

8. If you want to come to my house later, call _____.

9. These chairs are so heavy. It's hard for me to move _____.

10. I can't find my cell phone. Do you know where _____ is?

Part B Circle the letter of the answer that correctly completes each sentence.

1. The mountains are beautiful. In winter, _____ are covered with snow.

    (A) them   (C) it

    (B) we   (D) they

2. _____ need to buy a clock for the front bedroom.

    (A) He   (C) She

    (B) Me   (D) I

3. I love your glasses. Where did you buy _____?

    (A) it   (C) them

    (B) they   (D) your

4. Are you going to carry that big box by yourself? Do you need me to help _____?

    (A) me   (C) your

    (B) you   (D) it

5. My uncle is a lawyer. _____ lives in New York.

   (A) He   (C) Him

   (B) She   (D) Her

6. We want to know about today's special lunches. Can you tell _____ what they are?

   (A) us   (C) we

   (B) me   (D) them

7. Caroline loves sports. _____ likes tennis the best.

   (A) Her   (C) She

   (B) It   (D) They

8. Do _____ to drive you home?

   (A) I want you   (C) you want I

   (B) you want me   (D) we want she

9. My watch is broken. _____ needs a new battery.

   (A) It   (C) We

   (B) I   (D) They

10. If you see John and Jim, tell _____ to call _____.

    (A) me . . . they   (C) them . . . me

    (B) they . . . me   (D) I . . . them

Part C Underline the word that correctly completes each sentence.

1. (I, Me) need to study for tomorrow's test.

2. The students are happy because (them, they) have no homework.

3. Where did you park (you, your) car?

4. (We, Us) were happy when the doctor told (we, us) that (our, their) father is healthy.

5. Freddy sailed (him, his) boat across the Gulf of Mexico.

6. My sister ripped (she, her) shirt, so (she, he) sewed (her, it).

7. This is a difficult test, and (its, it) is very long.

8. I don't know where I put my keys. Did (your, you) see (they, them)?

9. Janet is an excellent cook. (Her, She) makes delicious spaghetti.

10. The new puppies are so cute! (They, Them) are brown and black.

TEST 36 Object Pronouns

Clear Grammar 2, Unit 7

Name _____   Date _____

Part A Read each sentence carefully. Look at the underlined part. If the underlined part is correct, circle C. If it is wrong, circle X, and write the correct form next to it. Five of the sentences are wrong.

C   X   1. <u>My mother and me</u> went to the park together. _____

C   X   2. The radio broadcaster is not afraid to give <u>his</u> opinion. _____

C   X   3. I'm happy because my boyfriend called <u>my</u> from Germany. _____

C   X   4. Squirrels eat nuts. <u>They</u> don't eat meat. _____

C   X   5. When Annie saw her father, she hugged <u>his</u>. _____

C   X   6. Just between <u>you and I</u>, I don't think this test is so difficult. _____

C   X   7. We took our books <u>with our</u> to the library. _____

C   X   8. Gina was shocked when the waitress gave <u>her</u> the bill. _____

C   X   9. Tim's girlfriend made a sweater for <u>him</u>. _____

C   X   10. If you are going to the store, please get some butter <u>for me</u>. _____

Part B Underline the word that correctly completes each sentence.

1. Our teacher told (we, us) to study for the test.

2. Home improvement stores often show people how to do (their, them) own repairs.

3. We invited Harry to come to the movie with (we, us).

4. You should try these cookies! I bought (their, them) at the bakery.

5. The window looked plain until Sam put some curtains on (him, it).

6. The little boys were nervous because the big dog was close to (they, them).

7. If you don't understand your homework, (I, me) can help (your, you).

8. I brought flowers to (my, me) mother and put (them, their) on the kitchen table.

9. When Mars is close to earth, you can see (its, it) on a clear night.

10. We learned about the planets in school. We had to memorize (they, their) names.

Clear Grammar 2

Part C Circle the letter of the answer that correctly completes each sentence.

1. _____ coach watches _____ swim.

   (A) Our . . . we   (C) Our . . . us

   (B) We . . . us   (D) We . . . our

2. Dean and Linda bought six donuts and ate _____ in _____ car.

   (A) them . . . they   (C) their . . . them

   (B) them . . . their   (D) their . . . they

3. Nina started running when _____ brother threw a water balloon at _____.

   (A) she . . . her   (C) her . . . she

   (B) her . . . her   (D) her . . . it

4. Matthew is helping Lori. Lori bought an entertainment center, and _____ is going to put her television in ____.

   (A) his . . . it   (C) him . . . its

   (B) he . . . its   (D) he . . . it

5. Ralph was disappointed to find out that _____ didn't win the contest.

   (A) him   (C) he

   (B) his   (D) it

6. David hurt _____ hand when _____ was trying to hang a picture.

   (A) his . . . him   (C) him . . . his

   (B) him . . . he   (D) his . . . he

7. The downtown area is charming. _____ streets are filled with unique shops.

   (A) It's   (C) Its

   (B) It   (D) They

8. Jose invests in real estate because _____ wants to make money from _____.

   (A) he . . . its   (C) his . . . its

   (B) he . . . it   (D) him . . . it

9. Rose looks great for _____ age. _____ is not a child anymore.

   (A) her . . . She   (C) she . . . Her

   (B) hers . . . Her   (D) hers . . . She

10. Paula said _____ can all meet at _____ house and drive to the game together.

    (A) us . . . her   (C) us . . . her

    (B) we . . . he   (D) we . . . her

© 2005 University of Michigan   *101 Clear Grammar Tests*   **TEST 36**   84

TEST 37 *One* and *Other*

Clear Grammar 2, Unit 8

Name _____ Date _____

Part A Fill in the blanks with one of these: *another one, the other one, other,* or *others.*

1. I have two sisters. One is tall, and ___the other one___ is short.

2. The Golden Gate Bridge and the Empire State Building are famous U.S. sights.
   ___Others___ are the Lincoln Memorial and the St. Louis Arch.

3. I brought you one glass of water. Tell me if you need ___another one___.

4. McDonald's is a popular fast-food restaurant. Burger King and Taco Bell are
   ___other___ popular places.

5. Some of the kittens are gray, and ___others___ are black. I'm not sure about
   the rest

6. After Nancy finished her cup of coffee, she bought ___another one___.

7. Of the two chairs in the living room, this chair is comfortable, but ___the other one___ is
   not.

8. Tony has only visited France, but he wants to visit ___other___ countries.

9. There are two hospitals in our city. This hospital is close to our house.
   ___The other one___ is far away.

10. I don't want you to share my secret with ___other___ people.

Part B Read the underlined part. If the part is correct, write C in the blank. If it is wrong, write the correction on the line. Five sentences are not correct.

_____ 1. I didn't like last night's movie. Did you like <u>it</u>? ___C___

___≠___ 2. I just baked some peanut butter cookies. Do you want <u>it</u>? ___one___

_____ 3. Most of the students took the test. <u>The other</u> were absent. _____

___C___ 4. There are three kinds of muffins available. One is chocolate, and <u>the others</u> are
   blueberry and lemon. _____

___C___ 5. Some children like to play outside, <u>but other children</u> like to play video games in
   the house. _____

_____ 6. If you need a towel, I think there's ~~it~~ _one_ in the closet. _____

✗ 7. I have read one play by Shakespeare, and I want to read <u>the other~~one~~</u> _another one_

_____

_____ 8. Q: "Did you see the sunset last night?"

A: "No, I didn't see <u>it</u>." _____

✗ 9. Nancy has three children. One is a girl, and <u>the other</u> are boys. _____

_____ 10. If you don't understand the homework, we can do <u>it</u> together. _____

Part C Underline the word or words that correctly complete each sentence.

1. One of the states with the hottest weather is Florida. (<u>Another</u>, Others) is Arizona.

2. Brad has two pets. One is a dog, and (<u>the other</u>, other) is a cat.

3. *Matt:* "I feel like having an apple."

   Laura: "I think there's (<u>one</u>, it) in the kitchen."

4. Some teachers give a lot of tests. (<u>Others</u>, The other) don't.

5. Jimmy Carter is one U.S. President. (Other, <u>The other</u>) presidents were Ronald

   Reagan and Bill Clinton.

6. Our family owns three cars. One is American, and (<u>the others</u>, others) are Japanese.

7. This sofa is heavy. Can you help me move (<u>it</u>, one)?

8. There are six donuts in the box. One is coconut, and (<u>the other</u>, others) donuts are

   lemon.

9. Some dogs are friendly, and (another, <u>others</u>) are not.

10. The library doesn't have the book I need, so I have to get (other, <u>another</u>) one.

Clear Grammar 2, Unit 8

Name _____   Date _____

Part A Circle the letter of the answer that correctly completes each sentence.

1. I need help reading this essay. I don't understand _____.

   (A) it   (C) one

   (B) other   (D) another

2. If you don't have a pencil, I will give you _____.

   (A) it   (C) one

   (B) other   (D) another

3. That muffin was delicious. I think I'll have _____One_____.

   (A) it   (C) one

   (B) other   (D) another

4. *Q:* "Are these your only children?"

   A: "No. I have _____ child at home."

   (A) others   (C) the others

   (B) other   (D) another

5. Lisa planted three bushes today. She's going to plant some _____ bushes tomorrow.

   (A) others   (C) the others

   (B) other   (D) another

6. Some flowers grow well in direct sunlight, but _____ need to be in the shade.

   (A) others   (C) other

   (B) it   (D) one

7. There are two very popular cities in California. One is Los Angeles, and _____ is San Francisco.

   (A) other   (C) the others

   (B) others   (D) the other

8. Some of the guests are in the kitchen, and _____ are in the living room.

   (A) other

   (B) others

   (C) the other

   (D) another

9. Katie read a beauty magazine and found _____ way to fix her hair.

   (A) other

   (B) others

   (C) the others

   (D) another

10. This is the only puzzle I've had trouble with. _____ were really easy.

   (A) The others

   (B) Another

   (C) The other

   (D) It

Part B Underline the word or words that correctly complete each sentence.

1. Susan and her husband have two cars. One is black, and (other, the other) is silver.

2. *Jean:* "Do you drink coffee very often?"

   Tom: "No. I don't really like (it, one)."

3. Ecuador and Venezuela are South American countries. (Others, Other) countries are Bolivia and Brazil.

4. Sheila didn't like any of the bracelets she saw, so the salesperson offered to show her some (others, the others).

5. Peter has two favorite subjects. One is grammar, and (another, the other) is vocabulary.

6. *Jill:* "I didn't bring my dictionary to school."

   Jack: "I brought both of mine. Do you want to borrow (it, one)?"

7. Ivan brought his new shirt to the store and exchanged it for (another, other) one.

8. The movie we planned to see was sold out, so we had to see (others, another) one.

9. If you don't get accepted to the university of your choice, there are (other, others) you can attend.

10. Edward is good at thinking of (other ways, others way) to solve a problem.

Part C Fill in the blanks with one of these: *one, it, another, other, others, the other,* or *the others.*

1. There are three chairs in the backyard. One is broken, but _the others_ are in good condition.

2. *Carl:* "I need a knife to open this box."

   Brad: "I think there's _one_ in the sink."

3. Harvey has two birds. One is green, and _the other_ is yellow.

4. There are six countries represented in our class. One country is Italy, and _another_ is Kuwait.

5. Margaret liked the first car she saw at the dealership, but she decided to look at _another_ one just to be sure.

6. There are a lot of things to do at summer camp. Swimming is one activity, and some _others_ activities include boating, hiking, and telling stories.

7. Julia couldn't carry all of her books at once, so she left _the others_ behind.

8. Michael needs a night light, so he went to the store to get _one_.

9. I think we should rent a movie. If you have _another_ idea, just tell me.

10. Ann has two favorite colors. One is blue, and _the other_ is purple.

TEST 39 Possessive

Clear Grammar 2, Unit 9

Name _____   Date _____

Part A Based on these conversational exchanges, fill in the blanks with the correct possessive pronoun.

1. *Q:* "Where are our cars?"

    A: "Mine is here, and ___yours___ is over there."

2. *Q:* "Where do Frank and Karen live?"

    A: "Do you see that house over there? It's ___theirs___."

3. *Jim:* "I'm so upset because my car isn't working."

    Mike: "We don't need our car today. You can borrow ___us___."

4. *Kelly:* "I'm so cold!"

    Sue: "If you don't have a sweater, you can borrow ___mine___."

5. *Tom:* "I think Linda left her phone here."

    Debra: "I think so, too. That phone looks like ___hers___."

6. *Q:* "Is this book ___yours___?"

    A: "No. Mine has a green cover."

7. John asked me to get his jacket, but I don't know which one is ___his___.

8. *Q:* "What's your middle name?"

    A: "___MINE___ is Beth."

9. *Mary:* "This is a great idea you have! Thanks for coming up with it!"

    Tim: "Actually, you should thank Mark for the idea. It was ___his___."

10. Jennifer is confused because she doesn't know which suitcase is ___hers___.

Part B Circle the letter of the answer that correctly completes each sentence.

1. _____ is in his garage.

    (A) The car of Barry   (C) The car Barry

    (B) Barry car   (D) Barry's car

2. Did you meet _____ when you went to his house?

    (A) James is father   (C) James' father

    (B) the father of James   (D) the father of James'

Clear Grammar 2

3. _____ is this?

   (A) Whose pencil   (C) Who's pencil

   (B) Whose pencils   (D) Who's pencils

4. I have two books, so you can _____ if you need to.

   (A) borrow mine   (C) borrow my

   (B) borrow your   (D) borrow me

5. _____ is an amazing aqua right now!

   (A) The sky's color   (C) The color of the sky

   (B) The color's sky   (D) The sky of the color

6. _____ baked cookies for us.

   (A) Elias' mother   (C) Eliases mother

   (B) The mother of Elias   (D) The mothers of Elias

7. _____ are we taking to the party?

   (A) Who's car   (C) Whose's car

   (B) Whose car   (D) Who is car

8. I lost my pen. Can I borrow _____?

   (A) you   (C) your

   (B) you're   (D) yours

9. _____ are an inch too long.

   (A) The shirts sleeves   (C) The sleeves of the shirt

   (B) The shirt of the sleeves (D) The sleeve's shirt

10. _____ did you use for the game?

   (A) Who's tennis racket   (C) Whose is tennis racket

   (B) Whose tennis racket   (D) The tennis racket of whose

Part C Combine the two sentences. Write the correct possessive form.

Example: Jeanine has a cat. It is fat. ___*Jeanine's cat is fat.*___

1. Beverly has a car. It is black. _____

2. Cindy has a wallet. It is in her purse. _____

3. Maria has a house. It is large. _____

4. Nancy has three children. They are in school. _____

5. Ali owns a watch. It is expensive. _____

6. Olga is married. Her husband is well educated._____

7. The teacher has a new shirt. It is blue. _____

8. The teacher collected the homework. The homework belongs to the students. _____

   _____

9. James has new sneakers. They are black and white. _____

10. Chris bought a new suit. It is too tight._____

TEST 40 Possessive

Clear Grammar 2, Unit 9

Name _____   Date _____

Part A Underline the words that correctly complete each sentence.

1. (Gloria's mother, The mother of Gloria) is coming to town next week.

2. (The color of my house, My house's color) is tan.

3. (Arthur's plan, The plan of Arthur) to drive across country required a lot of money.

4. People stood on (the top floor of a building, a building's top floor) to watch the

   parade.

5. *Q:* "(Whose, Who's) car is this? It's blocking my driveway."

   A: "It probably belongs to the people across the street. They're having a party."

6. (My parents, Mine parents) said that if my car doesn't start, I can use (their, theirs).

7. Our whole family attended (Nicole's graduation, the graduation of Nicole).

8. I need to remember to bring (my, mine) notes to school.

9. The (door of the oven, the oven's door) should be open when you are broiling food.

10. The (girl's, girls') restroom is out of order.

Part B Read each sentence carefully. If the underlined part is correct, circle C. If it is
wrong, circle X, and write the correct form on the line. Five of the sentences are wrong.

C   X   1. <u>Whose</u> going on the canoe trip this weekend? _____

C   X   2. The <u>childrens' room</u> is a mess. _____

C   X   3. <u>It's</u> going to rain soon. The sky is dark gray. _____

C   X   4. <u>Peggy's</u> favorite hobby is skydiving. _____

C   X   5. <u>The cars' trunk</u> doesn't lock. _____

C   X   6. <u>Who's</u> video camera are we going to bring? _____

C   X   7. Barry painted <u>the top of the table</u> bright blue. _____

C   X   8. We feed <u>ours</u> dog two times a day. _____

C   X   9. <u>Chris'</u> father is helping him build a model train. _____

C   X   10. The <u>actor's</u> name is Antonio Banderas. _____

Example: Arthur owns a television. The television is expensive.

_____*Arthur's television is expensive.*_____

1. The stereo is powerful. Robert owns the stereo.

   _____

2. Gregg owns a car. The car is purple.

   _____

3. Jan has a dress. The dress is colorful.

   _____

4. Peter owns the cell phone. His cell phone on the table.

   _____

5. Bobby owns a bicycle. The bicycle is blue.

   _____

6. Marsha has a pet rabbit. The rabbit is white.

   _____

7. The dolls are on the sofa. The dolls belong to Cindy.

   _____

8. The pens belong to the teacher. The pens are blue.

   _____

9. Bill has a dog. The dog is brown.

   _____

10. Fred has a boat. The boat is in the water.

    _____

Clear Grammar 2

TEST 41 Comparative and Superlative

Clear Grammar 2, Unit 10

Name _____   Date _____

Part A Underline the word or words that correctly complete each sentence.

1. Jack is short, but Jill is (more short, shorter).

2. This book is (more interesting, interestinger) than the last book I read.

3. Tony is (more smarter, smarter) than Don.

4. June is (the happiest, the most happy) person I know.

5. In my opinion, chocolate is good, but peanut butter is (better, gooder).

6. Nina runs (faster from, faster than) her sister.

7. The living room is cool, but the bedroom is (more cooler, cooler).

8. That is (the most ridiculous, ridiculousest) idea I've ever heard!

9. Frank is (the most intelligentest, the most intelligent) person I know.

10. Choosing a major in college is one of (the difficultest, the most difficult) decisions

    people make.

Part B Read the underlined part. If it is correct, write C in the blank. If it is wrong, write the correct answer next to it. Five sentences are not correct.

_____ 1. Francis hurt his leg, so he walks slowlier than other people. ____more____

_____ 2. College is more challenging than high school. _____

_____ 3. The weather in Georgia is bad, but the weather in Virginia is worse. __than__

_____ 4. This test is more easy than the last test. _____

_____ 5. We're all tired, but I think I'm the most tired. __than__

_____ 6. Ben is more hungrier than his brother. _____

_____ 7. Rabbits move more quickly than turtles. _____

_____ 8. Dulles Airport is more busy than National Airport. __busier than__

_____ 9. We have the best teacher! _____

_____ 10. My dog is fat, but my cat is more fat. __ter__

Part C Fill in the blanks with the correct comparative or superlative form of the word in parentheses.

Example: Nicole is interested in culture, but Tom is (interested).

_____more interested_____

1. My brother is (tall) _the tallest_ child in the room.

2. Diana is (lazy) _lazier than_ her brother.

3. Rhode Island is (small) _the smallest_ state in the U.S.

4. Texas is large, but Alaska is (large) _larger_ .

5. Alaska is (big) _the biggest_ state in the U.S.

6. Rachel is quiet, but Theresa is (quiet) _quieter_ .

7. My brother is (strong) _stronger than_ I am, and my father is (strong) _the strongest_ of all of us.

8. I bought (cheap) _the cheapest_ plane ticket available.

9. There were six lines at the airport. We tried to wait in (short) _the shortest_ one.

10. In math, division is (complicated) _more complicated than_ addition.

TEST 42 Comparative and Superlative

Clear Grammar 2, Unit 10

Name _____   Date _____

Circle the letter of the answer that correctly completes each sentence.

1. Laura has three children. She thinks her _____ child is _____.

   (A) oldest . . . the most creative   (C) older . . . the most creative

   (B) oldest . . . the more creative   (D) older . . . the more creative

2. For Terry, math is _____ science.

   (A) more challenging   (C) more challenging than

   (B) challenginger   (D) challenging than

3. My boyfriend is _____ I am during a crisis.

   (A) more calm   (C) more calmer than

   (B) calmer than   (D) calmest than

4. The Sears Tower is _____ building in Illinois.

   (A) tallest   (C) the tallest

   (B) taller   (D) the taller

5. Exercising regularly can be _____ part of staying in shape.

   (A) the most difficult   (C) the difficultest

   (B) the more difficult   (D) the difficulter

6. You need to be _____ with eggs than with potatoes.

   (A) more carefuller than   (C) more careful

   (B) more carefuller   (D) carefuller

7. The rooms downstairs are _____ the rooms upstairs.

   (A) coolest   (C) the coolest than

   (B) cooler   (D) cooler than

8. The bride said she couldn't be _____.

    (A) more happier   (C) most happy

    (B) most happier   (D) happier

9. Some people feel that being a parent is _____ job.

    (A) the most rewarding   (C) the rewardingest

    (B) most rewarding   (D) more rewarding than

10. Inez was eating alone, so she asked the grocer for a _____ piece of fish.

    (A) more small   (C) smaller

    (B) most small   (D) more smaller

Part B Fill in the blanks with the correct comparative or superlative form of the word in parentheses. Follow the example.

    Example: Alaska is (cold) ___*the coldest*___ state in the United States.

1. Jimmy is (silly) _____ boy on the playground.

2. Michelle didn't feel well yesterday, but she feels (well) _____ today.

3. Ashley is (talented) _____ her older brother.

4. Turtles move (slowly) _____ rabbits.

5. Sometimes after vacation people are (tired) _____ before they left.

6. With all the windows, our kitchen is (bright) _____ room in our house.

7. Oscar doesn't want to drive to the Italian restaurant because it is (far) _____ the Spanish restaurant.

8. This old chair is (comfortable) _____ piece of furniture in my house.

9. Roger is (nice) _____ person I know.

10. Ginny got (high) _____ score in the class.

Clear Grammar 2

Part C Underline the words that correctly complete each sentence.

1. Barbara bakes (the most delicious, deliciouser) cookies.

2. Don likes to use (the most sharp, the sharpest) pencil he can.

3. The movie theater is (more crowded, crowdeder) on Saturday than on any other night.

4. Dan likes (older, more old) furniture, but his son prefers (moderner, more modern) furniture.

5. Disney World is (most exciting, the most exciting) place for a child to visit.

6. If you plan to go outside, you should wear a (more heavy, heavier) jacket.

7. Mitchell is (the most serious, the more serious) member of our family.

8. Lena looked at some expensive cars, but she decided to buy a (cheaper, cheapest) one.

9. Diamonds are (the most strong, the strongest) stones in the world.

10. I thought yesterday was a bad day, but today is (more bad, worse)!

TEST 43 Modals

Clear Grammar 2, Unit 11

Name _____ Date _____

Part A Underline the word or words that correctly complete each sentence.

1. We (may, will) buy a new car, but we're not sure.

2. If you don't have enough money to fly, you (would, might) want to take a train.

3. Gene doesn't have enough time, so he (doesn't will, will not) go to the party.

4. It's raining outside, so you (should, should to) take a jacket.

5. (You can help, Can you help) me carry these bags?

6. If it doesn't rain, we (can, would) go to the park.

7. You (don't have to, must not) cheat on the test.

8. (You would like, Would you like) a soda?

9. Some drivers are turning their windshield wipers on. It (may, must) be raining.

10. You seem tired. You (ought to, should to) go to sleep.

Part B Circle the letter of the answer that correctly completes each sentence.

1. My plane leaves in five minutes! I _____ hurry!

   (A) could   (C) may

   (B) should   (D) had better

2. _____ a pencil or pen on this application?

   (A) Might I use   (C) I should use

   (B) Would I use   (D) Should I use

3. If I were you, I _____ for the test.

   (A) would prepare   (C) will prepare

   (B) ought to prepare   (D) may prepare

4. _____ the door for me, please?

   (A) Will you open   (C) You will open

   (B) Must you open   (D) May you open

5. When I was younger, I _____ French.

   (A) can not speak   (C) could not speak

   (B) will not speak   (D) had better not speak

6. You _____ me tonight, but you can if you want to talk.

   (A) must not call   (C) don't have to call

   (B) should to call   (D) don't can call

7. If you don't have a lot of money for traveling, you _____ with some friends and share expenses.

   (A) must goes   (C) should went

   (B) could go   (D) go might

8. _____ me your book?

   (A) Could you lend   (C) You could lends

   (B) Could you lends   (D) You must lend

9. Arthur _____ his wife to the doctor.

   (A) don't can drive   (C) must not to drive

   (B) can not drive   (D) should not drives

10. _____ English well?

    (A) Do your parents can speak   (C) Can your parents speaks

    (B) Your parents can speak   (D) Can your parents speak

Part C   Read the underlined part. If the underlined part is correct, write C in the blank. If it is wrong, write the answer on the line. Five sentences are not correct.

_____ 1. When Fred was five years old, he <u>can not spell</u> his name. _____*could not spele*_____

_____ 2. The meat is raw. The oven <u>must be</u> broken. _____

_____ 3. <u>Should you carry</u> these packages for me, please? _____*could*_____

_____ 4. <u>Would you like to come</u> to my house tonight? _____

_____ 5. Next Friday we <u>would go</u> to Europe. _____*will / are going to*_____

_____ 6. <u>I would like to take</u> a vacation. _____

_____ 7. <u>Do I may ask</u> you a question? _____*May I ask you*_____

_____ 8. If I had a million dollars, <u>I will quit</u> my job. _____*would quit*_____

_____ 9. We <u>could work</u> together to find a solution to the math problem. _____*should*_____

_____ 10. To enter a foreign country, you <u>must have</u> a passport. _____

TEST 44 Modals

Clear Grammar 2, Unit 11

Name _____ Date _____

Part A Unscramble the words to make sentences and questions. Write your new question or sentence on the line, and pay attention to punctuation. Follow the example.

Example: borrow please pencil may I a

_____May I please borrow a pencil_____ ?

1. I may paint sure the bedroom I'm this weekend but not

   May I paint the bedroom, but I'm not sure this weekend ?

2. I book share may with your you

   May I share your book with you ?

3. had you without not exercise drinking enough better water

   You had better not exercise without drinking enough water

4. we to find may bus be a seat able on the

   We may be able to find a seat on the bus.

5. you well you feel tonight better sleep tomorrow if should

   You should feel better tomorrow if you sleep well tonight

6. I closes get to must bank before the it

   I must get to the bank before it closes.

7. if I you would were my ask boss more money for I

   If I were you, I would ask my boss more money.

8. may in I school be tomorrow not

   I may not be in school tomorrow.

9. you me tell to me about call the will homework

   Will you call me to tell about the homework ?

10. I a boy I hold could my little breath for was two when minutes

    When I was a little boy, I could hold breath for two minutes

Part B Read each sentence carefully. Look at the underlined part. If the underlined part is correct, circle C. If it is wrong, circle X, and write the correct answer on the line. Six of the sentences are wrong.

C X 1. I <u>should to take</u> my dog for a walk. _____

C X 2. Our bird <u>will sleeps</u> when we cover its cage. _____

C X 3. Dennis <u>may not have</u> time to cook dinner when he gets home.

_____

C X 4. The teacher <u>doesn't will review</u> the homework in class.

_____

C X 5. My wife and I <u>may not be able to get</u> a loan for our home.

Should I save? _____

C X 6. <u>Do I should save</u> more money before I buy a car? _____

C X 7. You <u>must to have</u> a visa to stay in this country. _____

C X 8. <u>She can</u> sing well? _____

C X 9. Jordan told Emma that <u>he will be late</u> for the party. _____

C X 10. You <u>should</u> call your mother on her birthday. _____

Part C Match the first part of the sentence with the second part. Write the letter of the matching part in the blank. Follow the example.

_d_ 1. It must have rained last night   a. if your car doesn't start tomorrow.

_g_ 2. The museum might be closed,   b. I would like the ocean more.

_f_ 3. You had better not pet that dog   c. on Sunday.

_a_ 4. I can take you to work   d. because the ground is wet.

_h_ 5. Would you help me   e. because it looks dirty.

_c_ 6. The post office will be closed   f. because it looks dangerous.

_b_ 7. If I could swim,   g. but I'm not sure.

_e_ 8. You should vacuum your carpet   h. carry these books?

Part D Circle the letter of the answer that correctly completes each sentence.

1. Barry is an excellent dancer. He _____ dance to any type of music.

   (A) can (C) should

   (B) must (D) had better

2. Daniel has to pass his history test, so he _____ study every day.

   (A) may (C) will

   (B) might (D) could

3. There _____ be traffic on the roads. Let's listen to the traffic report and find out.

   (A) had better (C) might

   (B) must (D) should

4. Tom didn't buy any cream or sugar. He _____ to have coffee in the morning.

   (A) had better not to plan (C) should not to plan

   (B) must not plan (D) may plan

5. The electricity _____ go out because of the storm, so we _____ find some candles.

   (A) must . . . can (C) had better . . . could to

   (B) might . . . will to (D) may . . . should

6. _____ me in the morning and wake me up?

   (A) Would you call (C) Will you to call

   (B) Will you calling (D) Could you called

7. If I _____ afford a camera, photography _____ be my favorite hobby.

   (A) could . . . would (C) can . . . had better

   (B) would . . . will to (D) may . . . must

8. I _____ to return your money to you. I'll know for sure on Friday.

   (A) must to be able (C) may not be able

   (B) might to be able (D) may not able

9. There _____ be a lot of cars in the parking lot, so we _____ try to get to our car quickly.

   (A) may . . . must to (C) had better . . . may

   (B) should to . . . may not (D) will . . . should

10. I _____ what I saw on the news last night. It was very unusual.

    (A) no could believe (C) couldn't believe

    (B) could not to believe (D) could not believed

TEST 45   Problem Words

Clear Grammar 2, Unit 12

Name _____   Date _____

Part A   Underline the word or words that correctly complete each sentence.

1. I (am, have) hungry. Let's get something to eat.

2. I am (very, too) short to reach the items on the top shelf.

3. (There is, There are) some empty folders on my computer.

4. This room (have, has) two doors.

5. Police officers (carries, carry) guns for self-defense.

6. Be quiet. The baby is (almost, most) asleep.

7. It's important (to study, for study) a little bit every day.

8. Jose answered the teacher's question, and he (has, was) right.

9. I am (very, too) tired to wash the dishes tonight. I'll wash them tomorrow.

10. (There is, There are) a bowl of fruit on the kitchen table.

11. Doctors (have, are) great responsibilities at work.

12. Jody often (helps, help) Omar with his class work.

13. (Most, Almost) of the students are finished with their tests.

14. I called my friend (for, to) ask her about the day's assignments.

15. Brian is younger than Cheryl. He (has, is) 27 years old, and she is 28.

Part B   Read the underlined part. If the part is correct, write C in the blank. If the part is wrong, write the correct answer on the blank line. Seven sentences are not correct.

_____ 1. Keith went to the tennis court to practice his serve. _____

_____ 2. Peggy ate most of her breakfast. _____

_____ 3. These days cars uses less gas than they did 20 years ago. _____

_____ 4. There are white, fluffy cloud in the sky. _____

_____ 5. Jerry is too old to join the army. _____

_____ 6. The little girl wouldn't go into the dark room because she has afraid.
               _____

_____ 7. Janie was absent from class <u>for personal reasons</u>. _____

_____ 8. T.J. is <u>most an adult</u>, so his parents are giving him more responsibilities.

~~duck~~
_____

_____ 9. <u>The baby ducks follow</u> their mother around the pond. _the_ _babies du_

___ 10. This town <u>has</u> two universities and several community colleges. _____

___ 11. It is <u>very cold</u> outside, so you should wear gloves. _____

___ 12. Karen <u>has fun</u> when she's ice skating. _____

___ 13. There are <u>very many people</u> on the elevator for me to get on.

_____

___ 14. Every day <u>the students and the teacher listens</u> to the principal's announcements.

_____

___ 15. <u>Almost people</u> don't like to do poorly on tests. _____

TEST 46 Problem Words

Clear Grammar 2, Unit 12

Name _____   Date _____

Part A Circle the letter of the answer that correctly completes each sentence.

1. I didn't eat lunch, so I _____.

   (A) have very hungry   (C) am very hungry

   (B) have very hunger   (D) am very hunger

2. Jerry likes to drink _____ coffee.

   (A) too hot   (C) most hot

   (B) too very   (D) very hot

3. _____ 50 states in the United States.

   (A) There is   (C) There are

   (B) Have   (D) Has

4. _____ anyone from Peru in your class?

   (A) Have there   (C) Is there

   (B) Has there   (D) Are there

5. The average _____ 300 miles per hour.

   (A) airplane flies   (C) airplane fly

   (B) airplane is fly   (D) airplane has

6. _____ in the movie theater laughed out loud.

   (A) Almost the people   (C) Almost all of the people

   (B) Most the people   (D) Most all the people

7. Scientists are working hard _____ a cure for cancer.

   (A) for find   (C) to finding

   (B) to find   (D) for to find

8. Melissa _____ two children.

   (A) has   (C) is

   (B) have   (D) are

9. Cheryl _____ of horror movies.

(A) have afraid

(C) has afraid

(B) is afraid

(D) are afraid

10. Our new sofa is _____ to fit in the living room, so we have to return it.

(A) very big

(C) too big

(B) very too big

(D) most big

11. The U.S. flag _____ 13 stripes and 50 stars.

(A) has

(C) is

(B) have

(D) am

12. _____ a storm headed this way.

(A) There are

(C) Has

(B) There is

(D) Have

13. Manuel's sisters _____ visit him soon.

(A) are going

(C) are going to

(B) is going

(D) is going to

14. The exact number of stars _____ impossible to determine.

(A) has

(C) are

(B) is

(D) were

15. _____ dishes Arlene serves are made with chicken.

(A) Most of the

(C) Most the

(B) Almost of the

(D) Almost the

Part B Underline the word that correctly completes each sentence.

1. I think you (have, are) right. I think we don't have school on Friday.

2. Our math homework was (very, too) confusing, but we figured it out.

3. (There is, There are) no water in the dog's bowl.

4. (Does, Is) there a waiting list to buy football tickets?

5. George and Laura (lives, live) together in a large house.

6. (There are, Have) many dishes to wash before we go to sleep.

7. How many icons (are, does) there on your desktop?

8. The distance between Tampa and Miami (are, is) 265 miles.

9. Benjamin grew two inches last year. Now he's (most, almost) three feet tall.

10. Beth hired an accountant (to, for) help her with her taxes.

11. New York (has, is) a lot of sights to see.

12. On his next birthday, Roger will (have, be) 36.

13. Catherine didn't exercise (very, too) much this week, so she feels strange.

14. (Are, Do) there any new developments in the investigation?

15. The people in this city (likes, like) to stay out late on weekends.

TEST 47 Review of Book 2

Clear Grammar 2, Units 2–12

Name _____ Date _____

Part A Underline the word or words that correctly complete each sentence.

1. Stacey bought (a, an, the) new hat for her mother.

2. Brad and I (are going to go, are going to, going) to the park later.

3. (Did you see, Did you saw) the rainbow in the sky?

4. (How much, How many) days are there in this semester?

5. Carl (often falls, falls often) asleep while he's watching television.

6. If you find my notebook, please return it to (I, me, my).

7. Creative writing is one major available at this university. (Other, Others, Another) majors are psychology and engineering.

8. (Jessica's, Jessica, Jessicas') favorite color is deep purple.

9. Legal terminology is the (most difficult, difficultest) class I have.

10. Your tire is flat. You (had better, may, might) pull off the road.

11. I (have angry, am angry) because I made a foolish mistake on my test.

12. This classroom is (very, too) noisy. I can't study at all!

13. (Almost all, Most all) of the cake is gone.

14. (Almost, Most) people enjoy relaxing on the beach.

15. (A, An, The) United States is located just south of Canada.

16. When she was younger, Louise (is, was, are) tall for her age.

17. (How much, How many) money do you need before you can buy a car?

18. Maria (almost never exercises, never exercises almost) because she has knee problems.

19. (Chris', Chrises) best friend lives in Russia.

20. Fred's favorite food is sushi, but (my, me, mine) is pizza.

Part B Circle the letter of the answer that correctly completes each sentence.

1. I saw _____ dog near the street. _____ dog was small and thin.

   (A) the . . . A

   (B) a . . . The

   (C) a . . . An

   (D) the . . . An

2. Ryan and Patricia _____ to Paris for their honeymoon.

   (A) are going to

   (B) are go to going

   (C) are going to go

   (D) going to go

3. Selena _____ to school early this morning.

   (A) comes

   (B) came

   (C) come

   (D) was coming

4. _____ stars do you think there are in the sky?

   (A) How much

   (B) How far

   (C) How many

   (D) How often

5. Anna _____ her father to see how he is feeling.

   (A) calls often

   (B) is often calls

   (C) call often

   (D) often calls

6. "_____ should we drive to the beach?"

   "If you have gas in your car, let's take _____."

   (A) Who's car . . . yours

   (B) Whose car . . . yours

   (C) Who's car . . . you

   (D) Whose car . . . your

7. I have two favorite movies. One is *The Miracle Worker,* and _____ is *Finding Nemo.*

   (A) another

   (B) other

   (C) the others

   (D) the other

8. _____ aunt lives in California.

   (A) Mine

   (B) She

   (C) I

   (D) My

9. If you're not sure about a career, you _____ want to see a counselor.

   (A) should   (C) had better

   (B) might   (D) must

10. *Q:* "_____ your hair?"

    A: "I cut it every month."

    (A) How often you cut   (C) How often do you cut

    (B) How long you do cut   (D) How do you cut

Part C Read the underlined part. If the underlined part is correct, write C in the blank. If it is wrong, write the correct answer next to it. Ten sentences are not correct.

_____ 1. I bought a new car. <u>The</u> interior is gray. _____

_____ 2. Anthony <u>is going work</u> late tonight. _____

_____ 3. We looked out the window as the plane <u>flied</u> over the ocean. _____

_____ 4. <u>How much water</u> do you drink every day? _____

_____ 5. Howard <u>is always</u> in his computer room. _____

_____ 6. My brother's CD player works, but <u>my</u> doesn't. _____

_____ 7. One popular ice cream flavor is chocolate. <u>Another</u> is vanilla. _____

_____ 8. <u>Kevin's phone</u> was busy for hours. _____

_____ 9. This is <u>the boringest</u> novel I have ever read! _____

_____ 10. <u>I must not study</u> for my final test because I understand all the material. _____

_____ 11. <u>I have sad</u> because the semester is over. _____

_____ 12. <u>It is too hot</u> to cut the grass. I'll cut it tomorrow. _____

_____ 13. The wedding will begin soon. The bride <u>is almost ready</u>. _____

_____ 14. Farmers <u>grow a pineapple</u> in Hawaii. _____

_____ 15. Cedric and Jessie <u>are going to learn</u> to play guitar. _____

_____ 16. After I ate a lot of candy, I <u>feeled</u> sick. _____

_____ 17. <u>Kelly's mother's house</u> is close to the elementary school. _____

_____ 18. I just heard <u>the funniest</u> joke! _____

_____ 19. I <u>cook seldom</u> fancy dinners. _____

_____ 20. When you're finished with the painting, please give it to <u>my</u>. _____

Clear Grammar 2, Units 2–12

Name _____   Date _____

Part A Read these sentences. Ten of them are correct, and ten have a mistake. Circle the mistakes, and then write the correct form of the mistake. Write C if the sentence is correct.

1. There was a news report about a boat that was lost at sea. _____

2. Gas prices going to decrease over the summer. _____

3. Bradley catched a cold, so he has to take medicine. _____

4. How far it is from New York to California? _____

5. It seems that the sky is always clear when we go sailing. _____

6. Jay's mother allowed he to spend the night at a friend's house. _____

7. Whose soda is this? I can't tell if it's mine. _____

8. The lasagna was so delicious that I decided to have other piece. _____

9. For many people, Monday is the worst day of the week. _____

10. The train will not arrive on time because it left the last station late. _____

11. Tina was lucky that she car didn't stall on a deserted road. _____

12. It's raining out, so you should bring an umbrella. _____

13. It's a beautiful day today. A sun is shining, and the air is cool. _____

14. I teared my shirt on this nail, so I have to change it before we go out. _____

15. How hot does it get in Arizona? _____

16. We usually order several appetizers when we go out to dinner. _____

17. Before the baseball game, the people sang them national anthem. _____

18. There were two President Roosevelts in U.S. history. One was Franklin, and another was Theodore. _____

19. Some people believe that John Lennon was the most talented member of the Beatles.

    _____

20. Martin was very hungry, so he ate a dozen donuts. _____

Part B Underline the word or words (ø stands for nothing) that correctly complete each sentence.

1. (The, ø) President of the U.S. lives in Washington, DC.

2. Norman (likes, is liking) to take a walk each morning.

3. Charles (didn't understood, didn't understand) what the waitress said, so he asked her to repeat it.

4. (How often does, How often do) trains depart from this station?

5. Darren (is always, always is) on time to work.

6. My father asked (I, me) to take care of his house while he was away.

7. Which of these bowling balls is (your, yours)?

8. Arizona and New Mexico are hot states. (Others, Other) are Florida and Texas.

9. My brother is (the smartest, the smarter) person I know.

10. You (must not, don't have to) drive a car without a license.

11. (Almost, Most) cats don't like to be in water.

12. (The, A) Statue of Liberty is in New York.

13. Janet (is going to, is going to go) Hawaii for her birthday.

14. Linda (weared, wore) a long dress to the wedding.

15. (How deep, How much deep) is the Grand Canyon?

16. Although it is hot during the day, it (is usually, usually is) pretty cool at night.

17. It's our parents' 50th anniversary, so we sent (them, they) on a cruise to Alaska.

18. (Who's, Whose) going to bring the cake to the party?

19. *Titanic* is (the most sad, the saddest) movie I have ever seen.

20. The teacher (must, may) allow us to drop one grade, but we're not sure.

Part C Circle the letter of the answer that correctly completes each sentence.

1. Jason _____, so he's going to take a nap.

   (A) has sleepy   (C) is sleepy

   (B) does sleepy   (D) do sleepy

2. _____ you give me your advice about my problem?

   (A) Should   (C) Had better

   (B) Will   (D) May

3. Is Pluto _____ planet in the solar system?

   (A) smallest   (C) the smallest

   (B) the smaller   (D) smaller

4. Purple is one color in the rainbow. What is _____?

   (A) the other   (C) the others

   (B) another   (D) others

5. I think this dictionary is _____. _____ dictionary is smaller.

   (A) my . . . Your   (C) mine . . . Your

   (B) my . . . Yours   (D) mine . . . Yours

6. When I admired Becky's necklace, she offered to give _____ to _____.

   (A) it . . . me   (C) its . . . my

   (B) its . . . me   (D) it . . . mine

7. The grass always _____ when it rains a lot.

   (A) grows quicklier   (C) grows more quickly

   (B) grows more quick   (D) more quickly grows

8. _____ will we need to get to the airport?

   (A) How many time   (C) How much times

   (B) How much time   (D) How often time

9. _____ to sell your car?

   (A) You did decide   (C) You did decided

   (B) Did you decided   (D) Did you decide

10. My cat _____ kittens soon.

    (A) going to have   (C) is going to have

    (B) going have   (D) is haveing

TEST 49 Phrasal Verbs

Clear Grammar 3, Unit 2

Name _____ Date _____

Part A Match the phrasal verb on the left with its meaning on the right. Write the letter of the meaning on the line by the number.

_f_ 1. Could you please ask Juan to <u>call</u> me <u>back</u>?   a. end a relationship

_d_ 2. What time do you <u>pick</u> your children

     up from school?   b. leave the ground

                 c. wait

____ 3. When you <u>get through</u> working, give me a call.   d. get someone

_g_ 4. I <u>wake up</u> at 6:30 on weekdays.   e. become an adult

_c_ 5. Please <u>hold on</u> for a moment.   f. return a phone call

_e_ 6. I want my kids to <u>grow up</u> in a safe country.   g. stop sleeping

_b_ 7. The plane didn't <u>take off</u> on time.   h. return to the correct place

_a_ 8. Mari is going to <u>break up</u> with Hito.   i. exit

____ 9. <u>Get off</u> at the mall, and transfer to the   j. complete

     Number 15 bus.

____ 10. I'm going to wash the dishes and <u>put</u> them <u>away</u>.

Part B Circle the letter of the answer that correctly completes each sentence.

1. Before you turn your test in to the instructor, you should _____.

   (A) go it over   (C) go over it

   (B) look it up   (D) look up it

2. Britney Spears called off a concert recently because _____.

   (A) all of the tickets sold quickly   (C) she had a knee injury and couldn't perform

   (B) the musicians were playing well   (D) her cell phone was not getting a clear signal

3. When you drive through a school zone and the yellow light is flashing, you should

   _____.

   (A) slow down   (C) break down

   (B) hurry up   (D) give up

Clear Grammar 3

4. While Shuko was driving to work, her car ran _____ of gas.

    (A) out   (C) over

    (B) off   (D) away

5. In Japan, it's customary to take _____ your shoes before you enter someone's home.

    (A) out   (C) on

    (B) away   (D) off

Part C Read the meaning of the phrasal verb, and then fill in the blank with the missing word.

PHRASAL VERB	MEANING
1. find _____	get information about something
2. turn _____	increase the volume
3. look _____	take care of
4. keep _____	continue
5. eat _____	eat at a restaurant

Part D Read each sentence carefully. Look at the underlined part. If the underlined part is correct, circle C. If it is wrong, circle X, and write the correct form on the line. Two sentences are not correct.

C   X   1.   Before I buy new clothes, I always <u>try on them</u>. _____

C   X   2.   My sister is my best friend. I know I can always <u>count on her</u>. _____

C   X   4.   This geometry problem is tricky. I can't <u>figure out it</u>. _____

C   X   5.   I'm not feeling great. I had a bad cold last week, and I'm just

                   <u>getting over it</u>. _____

C   X   5.   It's cold out. You might want to <u>put your jacket on</u>. _____

Clear Grammar 3, Unit 2

Name _____   Date _____

Part A Add the correct word to complete these sentences using phrasal verbs.

1. Alice looked _____ the word *volume* because she wasn't familiar with it.

2. In April, it is necessary to figure _____ how much tax money you owe the government.

3. Beth heard a noise outside, so she woke her husband _____.

4. The court clerk handed _____ questionnaires to the panel of jurors.

5. It was very warm in the house, so Cheryl turned _____ the air conditioner.

6. Before moving out of his apartment, Zachary gave his key _____ to the landlord.

7. Donna picked her son _____ from school on her way to the gym.

8. When you're picking people _____ at the airport, it's best to find _____ if their plane is on time, before you got to the airport.

9. Yolanda forgot to put _____ the butter before she went to sleep, so it was completely melted in the morning.

10. Suzanne tried _____ 25 wedding gowns before she found the one she eventually bought.

Part B Circle the letter of the answer that correctly completes each sentence.

1. Wanda _____ a list of things to buy at the supermarket.

   (A) turned down   (C) wrote down

   (B) put back   (D) put on

2. Elaine was absent from school for five days, so she had to work hard to _____ the other students.

   (A) catch up with   (C) catch on to

   (B) watch out for   (D) check into

3. Vincent _____ an application for a job at the pizza place on the corner.

   (A) filled in   (C) filled up

   (B) filled with   (D) filled out

4. When swimming in the ocean, you need to _____ jellyfish that might float by.

   (A) catch up with   (C) come across

   (B) watch out for   (D) look up to

5. After the plane _____, the passengers were allowed to use their computers.

   (A) took off   (C) took up

   (B) turned off   (D) turned up

6. Nina tries to _____ going to the dentist because she is deathly afraid of pain.

   (A) put on   (C) cross off

   (B) wake up   (D) put off

7. When Donald and Ivana _____, she walked away with half his money.

   (A) broke down   (C) broke up

   (B) made up   (D) found out

8. Frances ate two bananas and then _____ the peels _____.

   (A) threw . . . away   (C) handed . . . out

   (B) left . . . out   (D) took . . . off

9. The passengers _____ the cruise ship in Miami and sailed to the Bahamas.

   (A) got along with   (C) got off

   (B) got over   (D) got on

10. Ben _____ his coat before he went outside to play in the snow.

   (A) put up with   (C) put on

   (B) took off   (D) turned on

Part C Underline the words that correctly complete each sentence.

1. The bus I was on (broke down, broke up), so we all had to (get over, get off).

2. My mother wasn't home when I called her the first time, so I (called her back, called her off) later in the day.

3. (Look after, Look out for) that pedestrian! You are going to hit him!

4. Tina tried to lose weight for a while, but then she got frustrated and (got up, gave up).

5. George borrowed his neighbor's lawn mower and promised to (give it away, give it back) in a week.

6. When we (ran into, ran out of) ice at our party, I sent my husband to the store to get more.

7. The receptionist asked Marcus to (hurry up, hold on) while she checked her appointment book.

8. The security guard (tried on, turned on) the lights when he arrived for work.

9. Most people hate having to (put up with, put on) dishonesty.

10. The students were told to (hand in, hand out) their essays to the teacher.

TEST 51 Past Progressive Tense

Clear Grammar 3, Unit 3

Name _____ Date _____

Part A Underline the verb form that correctly completes each sentence.

1. I (took, was taking) a shower when you (called, were calling me).

2. Karim (did, was doing) all his homework before dinner.

3. When Gabriela (met, was meeting) her husband, she (lived, was living) in Guatemala.

4. Dao (liked, was liking) her job at the restaurant.

5. (Did you were, Were you) waiting a long time at the bus stop?

6. Mr. Lee (planned, was planning) a trip around the world when he (lost, was losing) his job.

7. While she (waited, was waiting) for the bus, Jasmine (saw, was seeing) a car accident.

8. I (left, was leaving) some dinner in the oven for you.

9. (Did you enjoy, Were you enjoying) the movie?

10. While I (baked, was baking) cookies, my husband (washed, was washing) the car.

Part B Complete each sentence with either the simple past or the past progressive form of the verb in parentheses.

1. (attend)   In 1992, I attended a conference in Miami.

   When Hurricane Andrew hit Florida, I was a-ing a conference in Miami.

2. (sleep)   Mr. Winters was sleeping on the couch when his wife came home from work.

   He sleept on the couch until midnight.

3. (throw)   The boy was t-ing rocks at the abandoned house when the police arrived.

   The boy threw a rock at the police car!

4. (play)   My sister and her boyfriend p-ed video games last night.

   While my sister and her boyfriend were p-ing video games, I washed the

   dinner dishes and vacuumed the carpets.

5. (send)   Mai sent e-mails to all of her cousins yesterday.

   After she sent the last e-mail, her computer crashed.

TEST 52   Past Progressive Tense

Clear Grammar 3, Unit 3

Name _____   Date _____

Part A   Read each paragraph, and underline the words that correctly complete the paragraph.

1. Last week while I (listened, was listening) to the radio, I (heard, was hearing) about a popular online activity called blogging. I (didn't know, wasn't knowing) what it was, so I (asked, was asking) a friend of mine who is always surfing the Internet. She (explained, was explaining) that it means "web-logging" or writing a journal or diary online Then, she (showed, was showing) me some different blog sites that she likes to read.

2. Last year Samantha and Antonio (went, were going) to Japan for summer vacation. They (bought, were buying) rail passes and (traveled, were traveling) all over the country for one month, seeing the famous sights. At the end of their vacation, they (decided, were deciding) to hike Mt. Fuji. While they (hiked, were hiking), however, Antonio got a terrible stomachache. They (continued, were continuing) to hike, but his stomachache got worse, so they (returned, were returning) to the hotel. The next day, they went to a nearby hospital and discovered that Antonio had appendicitis. He (had, was having) surgery right away to remove his appendix. Three days later, while they (flew, were flying) home, they talked about what a memorable vacation it had been!

Part B   Read each sentence, and decide whether the correct tense for the verb in parentheses should be simple past or past progressive. Write the correct form of the verb in the blank.

1. (read)   While I _____ Friday's newspaper, I found an interesting article about a dog in Germany that knows 200 words.

2. (read)   Before I went to bed last night, I _____ a couple chapters of my psychology textbook.

3. (read)   While you _____, did you take notes?

4. (sleep)   At the time the earthquake hit, everyone _____.

Clear Grammar 3

5. (sleep)   We _____ very well after our long day at the beach.

6. (sleep)   I'm sorry to call so late. _____ you _____?

7. (work)   Enid _____ overtime every week in December.

8. (work)   While everyone else _____, Sean was talking on the phone to his girlfriend.

9. (work)   How many hours _____ you _____ last week?

10. (drop)   The child started crying when she _____ her ice cream cone.

Part C Answer these questions in complete sentences. Use the simple past or past progressive.

1. What were you doing last night at 8 P.M.?

_____

2. What did you do on your last vacation?

_____

3. What were you doing when you heard the news about Princess Diana's death?

_____

4. Which candidate did you vote for in the last election?

_____

5. The lights went out around midnight. What were you doing then?

_____

Clear Grammar 3

TEST 53 Present Perfect Tense

Clear Grammar 3, Unit 4

Name _____   Date _____

Part A Write the past participle for the following verbs.

1. be	was	_____	11. do	did	_____
2. work	worked	_____	12. hear	heard	_____
3. study	studied	_____	13. give	gave	_____
4. think	thought	_____	14. talk	talked	_____
5. tell	told	_____	15. break	broke	_____
6. write	wrote	_____	16. cook	cooked	_____
7. buy	bought	_____	17. fly	flew	_____
8. go	went	_____	18. read	read	_____
9. speak	spoke	_____	19. take	took	_____
10. drink	drank	_____	20. have	had	_____

Part B Fill in the blank in the simple past or present perfect tense of the verb in parentheses.

1. *Adeli:*   Hi, Sara. I know it's last minute, but do you and Martin want to go out for Chinese?

   Sara: (finish) Sorry, but we _____ just _____ dinner.

2. *John:*   (go) We're going to Thailand on vacation. My cousin _____ last year and said it's a beautiful and inexpensive country. _____ you _____ there?

   Manuel: (be) Yes, I _____ to Thailand two times. You'll love it!

3. *Vanita:*   (cook) _____ you ever _____ Indian food? It's delicious and healthy.

   Keiko: (make) Yes. I _____ chicken korma last night. It was easy and very tasty.

4. *Sandee:* I'm going to that salon called Haute Headz to get my hair cut today.

   Lisa: (get) _____ you _____ your hair cut there before? They're expensive.

   Sandee: (hear) No, I haven't, but I _____ that they do a great job.

5. *Debbie:* (try) _____ anyone ever _____ to swim from Key West to Cuba?

   Mike: (try) Not that I know of, but when I was a teenager, the mayor of Key West _____ to waterski the 90 miles from Key West to Cuba. He wasn't successful, though.

6. *Paul:* Did you like the movie?

   Raul: (see) No, not really. This is the second time I _____ it, and I still don't understand it.

   Paul: Really? I think it's the best movie I _____ so far this year.

7. *Passenger:* (leave) _____ the train _____ yet?

   Platform agent: (left) Yes, it _____ three minutes ago.

8. *Teacher:* (finish) _____ everyone _____ the assignment?

   Students: (finish) No, we _____ yet. Please give us a few more minutes.

9. *Monica:* (be) How long _____ you _____ married?

   Rimla: (be) I _____ married for 13 years. (get) We _____ married in 1991.

10. *Manabu:* (eat) Many foreigners _____ never _____ sushi before. Have you?

    Kevin: (eat) Yes, I _____ it many times. In fact, I _____ sushi last night at a Japanese restaurant near my house.

TEST 54 Present Perfect Tense

Clear Grammar 3, Unit 4

Name _____   Date _____

Part A Read the statement, and then write the verb in parentheses in the correct tense. Use simple past or present perfect. Follow the example.

> *Example:* (be) *Q:* "___*Have*___ you ever ___*been*___ to Germany?"
>
> *A:* "Yes. I was there for two weeks in June."

1. (win) *Q:* "_____ you ever _____ any contests?"

   A: "No, I haven't, but I don't compete much."

2. (begin) *Q:* "When _____ the movie _____?"

   A: "At 7:30. We're five minutes late."

3. (think) *Q:* "_____ you _____ about what you want for your birthday?"

   A: "Not really. I (have [neg]) _____ a lot of time."

4. (cost) *Q:* "How much _____ your outfit _____?"

   A: "Everything together, including the shoes, cost around $100."

5. (tell) *Mother:* "I _____ you a thousand times to put away your clothes!"

   Son: "I know, but I (forget) _____."

6. (drink) I _____ two glasses of chocolate milk five minutes ago, and now my stomach hurts.

7. (spent) After we _____ all of our money, we (decide) _____ to end our vacation.

8. (lose) Jeremy is frustrated because he _____ his keys twice so far this week.

9. (do) *Liz:* "I think I _____ too much work lately. I'm very tired."

   Mike: "I'm sure you are. You should take a day off."

10. (feel) The little boy _____ bad when his sister got in trouble for something he had done.

Part B Read each sentence carefully. Look at the underlined part. If the underlined part is correct, circle C. If it is wrong, circle X, and write the correct form on the line. Five of the sentences are wrong.

C   X   1.   Maria <u>has gone to</u> the hospital last week. _____

C   X   2.   Gina <u>ran</u> two miles so far. She has two more miles left to run. _____

C   X   3.   I <u>have been in bed</u> for two days. I can't seem to get over this cold. _____

C   X   4.   Arthur <u>has never seen</u> the Louvre Museum in Paris. _____

C   X   5.   Ross and Emily <u>has been</u> in London for two weeks. _____

C   X   6.   Kathy <u>doesn't left</u> for school yet, so she knows she's going to be late. _____

C   X   7.   Nancy <u>wore</u> a long white dress to her prom. _____

C   X   8.   <u>Have you already done</u> your homework? _____

C   X   9.   <u>I never forgot</u> the time I spent in the courtyard of Notre Dame. _____

C   X   10.   The students are nervous because they <u>haven't gotten</u> their grades yet. ____

Part C Circle the letter of the answer that correctly completes each sentence.

1. Edgar _____ his major when he was in his first year of college.

   (A) has chosen   (C) chose

   (B) have chosen   (D) is choosing

2. The athletes _____ well so far, but now they're having some problems.

   (A) has performed   (C) perform

   (B) have performed   (D) have performing

3. _____ anyone you know ever _____ to Europe?

   (A) Have . . . gone   (C) Did . . . gone

   (B) Has . . . gone   (D) Has . . . go

4. I'm exhausted. I _____ a good night's sleep in a week.

   (A) no have gotten   (C) didn't get

   (B) not have gotten   (D) haven't gotten

5. How long _____ your best friend?

   (A) did you know   (C) have you known

   (B) do you know   (D) are you knowing

6. I don't want to go swimming right now. _____ a heavy lunch.

   (A) I've just eaten   (C) I've eaten just

   (B) I'm just eaten   (D) Just I've eaten

7. Janice _____ a French class, but she's interested in signing up for one.

   (A) didn't take   (C) has never taken

   (B) has ever taken   (D) hasn't never taken

8. Sam is from Japan, but he _____ in the United States since 1990.

   (A) lived   (C) have lived

   (B) has been lived   (D) has lived

9. _____ breakfast yet?

   (A) You have eaten   (C) Have you eaten

   (B) Did you eaten   (D) Did you eat

10. Quitting his job was the worst decision Gary _____.

   (A) have ever made   (C) ever made

   (B) ever makes   (D) has ever made

TEST 55 Adverbs of Manner (-*ly*, *by*, *with*) and Related Terms

Clear Grammar 3, Unit 5

Name _____   Date _____

Part A Underline the adjective or adverb form that correctly completes each sentence.

1. I speak (slow, slowly) when I talk to someone who is learning my language.

2. Liz gave a presentation in class today. She did (good, well).

3. Even though he ran (fast, fastly), he still lost the race.

4. We stayed in a (love, lovely) little hotel in Paris. It was on a (quiet, quietly) street near Notre Dame.

5. I feel (bad, badly) because I never understand what Mrs. Carter is saying. She should speak more (clear, clearly).

6. Thu's family traveled around Germany (by, with) train.

7. The students improved their grades (by forming, to form) a study group.

8. You will get a (poor, poorly) credit rating (by don't paying, by not paying) your bills on time.

9. Did you know that you can make a telephone (by, with) two paper cups and a piece of string?

10. Sometimes tough situations require (creative, creatively) solutions.

Part B Underline the seven errors in this paragraph.

   When my car does not start in the morning, I have to go to the office by the bus. I am always lately because the bus is slow and makes a lot of stops. When I get to the office, I have to run to my desk and check my e-mail. Usually I can do it easy, but sometimes I don't enter my password correct because I type too quick. I try hardly to stay calm, but I get upset. I know that it will not be a well day for me.

Clear Grammar 3

TEST 56 Adverbs of Manner (-*ly*, *by*, *with*) and Related Terms

Clear Grammar 3, Unit 5

Name _____   Date _____

Part A Underline the adjective or adverb form that correctly completes each sentence.

1. In Florida, it often rains (hard, hardly) in the summer. These summer rainstorms usually start and finish (sudden, suddenly).

2. Some people get a headache if they eat ice cream too (quick, quickly).

3. I was very (nervous, nervously) about speaking in front of so many people.

4. Please be very (careful, carefully) driving home in this storm.

5. The tiger crouched (quiet, quietly) in the bushes until the deer was close.

6. A good teacher is (patient, patiently) and explains everything (clear, clearly).

7. I passed the driving test (easy, easily) the first time because I am a (good, well) driver.

8. All of the students hope to become (fluent, fluently) English speakers.

9. Leonardo works (good, well) alone and with a team.

10. In the U.S., it's (important, importantly) to arrive (prompt, promptly) for appointments.

11. Could you please turn down the TV? It's too (loud, loudly).

12. The girls talked (excited, excitedly) about the party on Friday night.

13. The 17-year-old tennis player from Russia played a very (strong, strongly) match.

14. Driving (careless, carelessly) can cause accidents.

15. Although Sanjay apologized (polite, politely) for being late, his girlfriend was (angry, angrily).

Part B Fill in the blanks with one of these words: *by, with,* and *to.*

1. Susan and Sven use coupons and shop at discount stores _____ save money.

2. The burglar got into their house _____ breaking a basement window.

3. *Tim:* This picadillo is delicious. How is it made?

   Sue: _____ ground beef, onions, tomatoes, olives, and raisins.

4. In Japan, people usually eat _____ chopsticks.

5. _____ comparing prices before you buy something, you can usually save money.

6. Sylvia wrote a letter to her landlord _____ complain about the leaky roof.

7. Sam was able to open the locked car door _____ a wire hanger.

8. My dream trip is to travel _____ train across China, Mongolia, and Russia.

9. The best way to learn a language is _____ studying and practicing it every day.

10. In ancient times, before people had watches, they told the time _____ sundials, candle clocks, and water clocks.

TEST 57   Prepositions after Verbs and Adjectives

Clear Grammar 3, Unit 6

Name _____   Date _____

Part A Fill in the blank with the correct preposition from the word box. Prepositions may be used more than once.

about	at	of	for	to	with

1. New Orleans is famous _____ delicious pastries called beignets.

2. Sejel writes a letter _____ her parents every week.

3. I am afraid _____ big spiders.

4. Jeff is always complaining _____ something.

5. That song reminds me _____ my trip to Brazil.

6. We are waiting _____ the rain to stop so we can go to the beach.

7. Mr. and Mrs. Jordan looked _____ ten houses but did not like any of them.

8. The defendant and his lawyer did not agree _____ the jury's decision.

9. We're waiting _____ bus 38.

10. I love to listen _____ the sound of falling rain late at night.

Part B Underline the words that correctly complete the paragraph.

My nephew is married (to, with) a woman that he met on a flight to Singapore. She (used to, was used to) work for a cruise line, and then she became a flight attendant. She was accustomed (of, to) traveling around the world. My nephew was an office manager and was ready (for, with) a change in his life. He was very interested (about, in) visiting new places, so he quit his job and became a flight attendant too. After three years of traveling and working together, they decided to get married. Now they are looking forward (at, to) the birth of their first child. I am very excited (about, for) having a new baby in the family!

TEST 58 Prepositions after Verbs and Adjectives

Clear Grammar 3, Unit 6

Name _____   Date _____

Part A Underline the preposition after the verbs or adjectives that correctly completes each sentence.

1. *A:* Thanks (to, for, with) helping me move in to the new apartment.

    B: No problem. You can count (on, for, with) me anytime you need help.

2. *A:* I always look forward (on, in, to) Thanksgiving every year. It's my favorite holiday.

    B: I agree (of, with, about) you. It's the least commercial and most relaxing holiday.

3. *A:* You must be very proud (of, to, for) Shima for getting accepted to Oxford

    University.

    B: We are, and we know that she'll be successful (for, in, of) her studies there.

4. *A:* Are you ready (to, of, for) the test?

    B: No. I'm far (of, from, with) ready!

5. Europeans are crazy (for, with, about) soccer, while Americans prefer football

    or baseball.

6. Jamie is thinking (to, of, for) moving to Los Angeles to pursue an acting career.

7. *A:* Did your parents approve (of, in, about) your marriage at such a young age?

    B: They were opposed (of, to, about) it at first but eventually accepted it.

8. *A:* Spaghetti again? I'm so sick (in, of, from) it!

    B: Me too. Let's talk (to, of, about) your brother about making something different

    tomorrow.

9. Our psychology professor reminds me (for, about, of) Einstein, with his thick

    white hair.

10. *A:* What happened (for, to, at) Karla? She looks really upset.

    B: Her husband forgot (about, from, for) their anniversary!

Part B Complete each sentence by adding the correct preposition and then completing the idea. Pay attention to the adjective or verb in the following clauses. Follow the example.

Example: Smoking is harmful ___*to your health*___ .

1. I'm good _____.

2. Egypt is famous_____.

3. I feel very satisfied _____.

4. I am interested _____.

5. When I was a child, I used _____.

6. I am scared _____.

7. I sometimes worry _____.

8. I am responsible _____.

9. Are you happy_____?

10. Now I'm finished _____.

101 Clear Grammar Tests **TEST 58**

Clear Grammar 3

TEST 59 Passive Voice

Clear Grammar 3, Unit 7

Name _____   Date _____

Part A Fill in the blanks with the correct passive voice forms.

1. The store will prosecute shoplifters. Shoplifters *will be* prosecuted.

2. The manufacturer recalled the defective toys. The defective toys *were recalled*

3. You must keep your dog on a leash. Dogs *must be kept* on a leash.

4. We have changed the date of the meeting to next Wednesday. The date of the meeting *has been changed* to next Wednesday.

5. Someone donated a painting by Picasso to the museum. A painting by Picasso *was donated* to the museum.

6. Most customers request a table in the nonsmoking section of the restaurant. A table in the nonsmoking section of the restaurant *is requested* by most customers.

7. The teacher has posted the exam grades on the class website. The exam grades *have been posted* on the class website.

8. Workers should finish construction of the new highway by next year. Construction of the new highway *should be finished* by next year.

Part B Underline the word or words that correctly complete each sentence.

1. Anya (born, <u>was born</u>) in Poland.

2. Who (<u>built</u>, was built) the pyramids in Egypt?

3. The new shopping mall (scheduled, <u>is scheduled</u>) to open in three months.

4. The amusement park has a new roller coaster. It is very (excited, <u>exciting</u>).

5. I am (tired, <u>tired of</u>) studying for the test.

6. Paolo's parents were (<u>shocked</u>, shocking) when he quit his job.

7. The name of the new president of the company (will announce, <u>will be announced</u>) next Friday.

8. The children enjoyed the (fascinated, <u>fascinating</u>) exhibits at the science center.

101 Clear Grammar Tests **TEST 59**   135

Clear Grammar 3

9. Many people (died, were died) when the building collapsed.

10. The (surprised, surprising) election result (posted, was posted) on websites all over the world.

11. Although construction ended in 2001, an official name for that collection of buildings (was, were) not decided until 2004.

12. Mrs. Wilson finally (agreed, was agreed) with me to purchase a (handpainted, handpainting) dish for each of the guests.

Name _____   Date _____

Part A Fill in the blanks with the passive voice form. Follow the example.

Example: Bell <u>invented</u> the telephone in 1876.

The telephone ___*was invented*___ by Bell in 1876.

1. The interviewer said that they <u>would call</u> me if I were selected for the job.

   The interviewer said that I *would be called* if I were selected for the job.

2. A tow truck <u>was towing</u> Luisa's car away when she arrived at her parking spot.

   Luisa's car *was being towed* away when she arrived at her parking spot.

3. We <u>clean</u> the bathrooms twice a week.

   The bathrooms *is cleaned* twice a week.

4. Cici and Clark <u>are going to build</u> their new house next year.

   Cici and Clark's new house *is going to be built* next year.

5. The deli <u>prepares</u> its food fresh each day.

   The deli's food *is prepaired* fresh each day.

6. Khalil Gibran <u>wrote</u> the book *The Prophet.*

   The Prophet *was written* by Khalil Gibran.

7. Governments <u>should provide</u> reasonably priced health care to their people.

   Reasonably priced health care *should be provided* by governments to their people.

8. In the 1700s, the British <u>used</u> the word "ain't" as part of standard English.

   In the 1700s, the word "ain't" *was used* by the British as part of standard English.

9. Sam <u>was</u> still <u>cooking</u> dinner when the guests started to arrive.

   Dinner *was* still *being cooked* when the guests started to arrive.

10. People of all cultures <u>have celebrated</u> the arrival of the New Year since ancient times.

    The arrival of the New Year *has been celebrated* by people of all cultures since ancient times.

Clear Grammar 3

Part B Read each sentence carefully. Look at the underlined part. If it is correct, circle C. If it is wrong, circle X.

C (X) 1. I <u>was</u> very <u>interesting</u> in insects and reptiles when I was a child.

C (X) 2. In some countries, food <u>is eating</u> with chopsticks instead of a fork.

(C) X 3. You must <u>be exhausted</u> from your long drive.

(C) X 4. Orlando's parks and tourist attractions <u>are crowded</u> on holidays.

C X 5. The Japanese language <u>writes</u> left to right or top to bottom.

C X 6. A bandage should be applied <u>by someone</u> to your laceration.

C X 7. The dry cleaning is ready, but your shirts <u>haven't been ironed</u> yet.

C X 8. The directions that came with the DVD player were very <u>confused</u>.

C X 9. Sugar cane <u>was grown</u> in large quantities in Florida many years ago.

C X 10. Much of the work at the homeless shelter is done <u>by unpaid volunteers</u>.

Part C Fill in the blank with the correct preposition after the past participles.

1. Are you satisfied __with__ your progress in the English course?

2. You look so much alike. Are you related __to__ each other?

3. We tried that new restaurant and were very impressed __with__ the food and service.

4. I am a little confused __about__ the assignment.

5. Pham was disappointed __with__ her test score.

Name _____   Date _____

Part A Underline the words that correctly complete the paragraph. In some cases, more than one correct answer might be possible.

On Friday nights my family likes to go to a restaurant (that, <u>which</u>, who) is near our home. The woman (that, which, <u>who</u>) owns the restaurant is from a town in Thailand (that, which, who) is near the Laotian and Cambodian borders. The meals (that, <u>which</u>, who) she serves represent the traditional foods of her homeland, as well as the foods (that, which, who) were brought to her town by people from neighboring countries (that, which, who) had to leave their homes during the Vietnam War. She learned to cook many types of food and brought all of the recipes with her when she came to the U.S. My family feels sorry for the people (who's, <u>whose</u>) lives were affected by the war, and we are honored to have the opportunity to eat delicious international meals (that, which, who) are available so close to our home.

Part B Create a sentence with a relative clause in it by including the second sentence in the first sentence. Use an appropriate pronoun.

1. My son is coming home for Thanksgiving. My son lives in Boston.
   My son, who lives in Boston, is coming home.

2. The leather jacket was on sale. Kayla bought it.
   The leather _____

3. The new reality show was filmed in Puerto Rico. Have you seen the show?
   _____

4. Marina baked the pumpkin pie. Everyone enjoyed the pumpkin pie.
   _____

5. The dance club used to be a train station. You should go to the dance club.
   _____

6. The security guard knows my brother. The security guard helped me when I locked my keys in my car.

   _____

7. You needed the money to pay your tuition. Did your parents send you the money?

   _____

TEST 62   Relative Clauses

Clear Grammar 3, Unit 8

Name _____   Date _____

Part A   Read the passage. Fill in the missing word or words: *who, whom, which, that, ø.*
(Indicate all possible answers, including ø for places where nothing is also correct.)

Several years ago, I traveled to Greece and spent a month-long vacation

❶ _____ I'll never forget. I traveled there with four friends ❷ _____ I had

known since college. We flew into Athens, and after spending three days there, took a

ferry boat to an island called Folegandros. It's a small island ❸ _____ is not well-

known by tourists. We stayed at a small hotel ❹ _____ was owned by an older

couple ❺ _____ daughter lived in Chicago. When we were hungry, we walked

to a nearby seaside café ❻ _____ served iced coffee and homemade yogurt with

honey for breakfast. In the late afternoons, we often sat in the café playing

backgammon and watching the fishermen unload everything ❼ _____ they had

caught. Then, for dinner, we would have fresh grilled calamari or fish ❽ _____

the fishermen had sold to the café. The café owner, ❾ _____ was a middle-aged

man with a large mustache, would often take a guitar-like instrument and play tradi-

tional Greek music for his customers.

After a wonderful week in Folegandros, we took a ferry boat to another island

called Amorgos, which has a beautiful mountain monastery ❿ _____ was shown

in the movie *The Big Blue*. On Amorgos, we stayed in a town ⓫ _____ was

located at the top of a mountain, and every day we walked the winding dirt roads

⓬ _____ led to old churches, ruins, and beaches. On our last day there, as we

were walking in the hot sun to the ferry station, a small truck passed by, driven by

two old men ⓭ _____ offered us a ride. We accepted immediately and jumped

into the back of the truck, where we noticed the other passengers—two sheep

⓮ _____ didn't look very happy to see us. As the truck bumped along the road,

© 2005 University of Michigan   *101 Clear Grammar Tests* **TEST 62**   **141** the sheep bumped into us, and about 30 minutes later, we reached the ferry boat station. We were windblown and smelled like sheep, but we thanked the two men for their help, bought our ferry tickets, and took the boat that afternoon back to Athens, full of laughter and smiles.

If you want vacation memories **15** _____ will last for a lifetime, I recommend the small, less-visited islands of Greece.

Part B Combine the sentences using *that, which, who, whom,* or *whose.* Follow the example. (In some cases, multiple answers may be possible.)

Example: I talked to a realtor about the house on Elm Street. The house is for sale.

_____*I talked to a realtor about the house on Elm Street that (which) is for sale.*_____

1. My cousin is a dentist. She works with very young children.

   _____

2. People will make more money over their lifetime than non-college graduates. They graduate from college.

   _____

3. The employees are very happy. Those employees got raises.

   _____

4. I always mix up the two words *por* and *para. Por* and *para* mean *for* in Spanish.

   _____

5. My cousin lives from Cartagena, Colombia, which is a beautiful old city. The city is surrounded by castle walls and looks like a bigger version of St. Augustine, Florida.

   _____

TEST 63 Infinitives and Gerunds

Clear Grammar 3, Unit 9

Name _____   Date _____

Part A Circle the form of the verb that correctly completes each sentence.

1. My little sister enjoys (to sleep, (sleeping)) in a tent in the backyard.

2. Would you like to go (to bowl, (bowling)) on Saturday?

3. The owners agreed ((to sell), selling) their house to us.

4. My brother is tired of (to work, (working)) the night shift.

5. Yuelong expects ((to graduate), graduating) from college in two years.

6. We couldn't afford to fly to California, so we thought about (to drive, (driving)) there.

7. Last year I forgot my cousin's birthday, but this year I remembered ((to buy), buying) him a gift.

8. Jeffrey's doctor advised him ((to get), getting) more exercise.

Part B Find the error in the underlined part of each sentence. Write the correction on the line.

1. My boss <u>would like me work</u> more hours.   *to*

   _____

2. Last year my parents persuaded my brother <u>to stopped smoking</u>.

   _____ *to stop* _____

3. The boy's mother <u>said him to put</u> his toys away.

   _____ *told him to put* _____

4. I <u>want that you show</u> me how to rollerblade.

   _____ *want you to show* _____

5. My friends <u>invited me to goes</u> to the beach on Saturday.

   _____ *to go* _____

6. I <u>look forward to meet</u> my roommate's parents.

   _____ *to meeting* _____

7. Our teacher <u>wants us finishing</u> our projects by next week.

   _____ *to finish* _____

8. If you <u>want me help</u> you with that work, call me. _____

   _____ *to help you* _____

TEST 64 Infinitives and Gerunds

Clear Grammar 3, Unit 9

Name _____   Date _____

Part A Underline the correct form—infinitive or gerund. If both are possible, underline both.

1. When people say their wedding vows, they promise (to love, loving) each other faithfully.

2. If you get migraine headaches, you should avoid (to eat, eating) common trigger foods such as chocolate, Chinese food, etc.

3. We invited Mike and Nancy (to come, coming) to the party on Friday.

4. Even though Terry's doctor told him (to stop, stopping) (to smoke, smoking), he has kept on (to do, doing) it.

5. Fatima would like (to go, going) to Greece on their next vacation, but her husband Abdul wants (to go, going) to London to visit relatives.

6. "If you continue (to drink and drive, drinking and driving)," Emma's friend warned her, "sooner or later, you will cause an accident and maybe kill yourself or someone else." Then she offered (to get, getting) Emma a taxi home.

7. Most American kids look forward to (have, having) the whole summer off from school.

8. Wan agreed (to watch, watching) his action movie if he would watch her romance movie afterward.

9. I suggest (to shop, shopping) around for the best deal before you make any big purchases.

10. When Inez and her fiancé decided (to postpone, postponing) the wedding, their families and friends couldn't help (to wonder, wondering) why.

11. We love to go (to camp, camping) in the mountains of Georgia in the fall.

12. Have you always liked (to learn, learning) about different countries and cultures?

13. When visiting Egypt or any Islamic country, women should avoid (to wear, wearing) shorts and sleeveless shirts.

14. When I was a child growing up in the Florida Keys, believe it or not, I got tired of (to have, having) fish and lobster so often!

15. When you get through (to clean, cleaning) your room, you can watch TV or play.

Part B Answer the following questions.

1. What is more commonly used as the subject of a sentence: a gerund or an infinitive?

   _____

   Write an example sentence:

   _____

2. What verb form (infinitive or gerund) is used after a noun or pronoun to tell or ask someone to do something, as in the following example: I want Mike (to go, going) to the bank. _____

3. List five other verbs besides *want* that are often followed by a noun/pronoun and tell or ask someone to do something.

   _____

4. Write a common error that you used to make with this grammar point before you studied this lesson.

   _____

   _____

Clear Grammar 3, Unit 10

Name _____   Date _____

Part A Look at the chart. Write 12 sentences about the people and the information. Four sentences should be affirmative, four should be negative, and four should be half affirmative and half negative to show contrast. Use these connectors: *and . . . too, and so . . . , and . . . either, and neither . . . ,* and *but . . . .*

Action/Situation	Keiko (female)	Hassan (male)	Ricardo (male)	Stanimira (female)
likes to dance salsa	No	No	Yes	No
has been to Indonesia	Yes	No	Yes	Yes
is a college student	Yes	Yes	No	No
drives a new car	Yes	No	Yes	No
loves ice cream	Yes	Yes	No	Yes
can speak three languages	No	Yes	No	Yes
is an outgoing person	No	Yes	Yes	No
can surf	Yes	No	No	No
is going to move soon	Yes	No	No	Yes

Affirmative

1. _____

2. _____

3. _____

4. _____

Negative

1. _____

2. _____

3. _____

4. _____

Contrast affirmative-negative or negative-affirmative

1. _____

2. _____

3. _____

4. _____

Part B Complete these sentences with these connectors: *to, in order to, for, however, therefore,* and *so.*

1. I'm going to the supermarket ___to___ buy some bread and orange juice.

2. Heinrich is studying Spanish _in order to_ apply for a position at his company's Madrid office.

3. Well, I have a lot of homework to do, ___so___ I guess I'd better get off the phone.

4. More and more organ transplants are done every year in the U.S. _however_, they are still complicated operations which carry serious risks.

5. Andrew asked a friend ___for___ assistance with the chemistry project.

6. _In order to_ get your best score on the TOEFL test, you should start studying and taking practice tests well in advance of your test date.

7. Most of the movie critics and my friends said the movie was terrible. _Therefore_, I decided not to waste my money seeing it.

8. The waiter came back to our table frequently _in order to_ refill our soft drinks.

9. When you called, I was just getting ready ___for___ work, ___so___ I couldn't talk for very long.

10. It's popular today ___to___ hire "clutter" consultants or coaches to help you clean up your home or office.

TEST 66 Connectors

Clear Grammar 3, Unit 10

Name _____   Date _____

Part A Underline the word or words that correctly complete each sentence.

1. Jean traveled to France (to, for, in order) learn about French culture.

2. Brandon took his date to an Italian restaurant (to, for, in order to) dinner.

3. Nicholas enjoyed the party, and I (enjoyed, did, so) too.

4. Henry doesn't like to dance, and (either, neither, so) does Barry.

5. Clark wants to go to the beach; (however, so, therefore), he has a lot of homework
   to do.

6. The students formed a study group (however, therefore, so) they could prepare for the
   test.

7. The movie was sold out. (So, However, Therefore), we had to see a different one.

8. Frank's refrigerator is broken, and (either, neither, so) is his oven.

9. Tomo has never been to Disney World, and (either, neither, so) has Hisaya.

10. The little boy sat on his father's shoulders (so, in order to, for) see the parade as it
    passed.

neither do I / so do I

Part B Write the second part of the sentence using connectors. Write both possible
answers. Follow the examples.

   Example: Alfred is good at fixing cars. Gary is good at fixing cars.

   Alfred is good at fixing cars, __*and so is Gary.*__

   Alfred is good at fixing cars, __*and Gary is too.*__

1. Don doesn't like football. Tyler doesn't like football.

   Don doesn't like football, _and neither does Tyler._____.

   Don doesn't like football, _and Tyler doesn't either_____.

2. Ice is kept in the freezer. Ice cream is kept in the freezer.

   Ice is kept in the freezer, _and so is ice cream._____.

   Ice is kept in the freezer, _and ice cream is too_____.

3. Rob watches a lot of scary movies. Ann watches a lot of scary movies.

   Rob watches a lot of scary movies, _and so does Ann_.

   Rob watches a lot of scary movies, _and Ann does too,_.

4. Marshall doesn't work on the weekend. His wife doesn't work on the weekend.

   Marshall doesn't work on the weekend, _and neither does his wife_.

   Marshall doesn't work on the weekend, _and his wife doesn't either_.

5. June is in the United States. Her family is in the United States.

   June is in the United States, _so is her family_.

   June is in the United States, _and her family is too_.

6. Leslie isn't home right now. Her daughter isn't home right now.

   Leslie isn't home right now, _and neither is her d._.

   Leslie isn't home right now, _and her d isn't either_.

7. Charlie eats a lot of chocolate. His Grandpa Joe eats a lot of chocolate.

   Charlie eats a lot of chocolate, _and so does his G_.

   Charlie eats a lot of chocolate, _and his G does too_.

8. Edna voted in the last election. Her husband voted in the last election.

   Edna voted in the last election, _and her husband did too_.

   Edna voted in the last election, _and so did her h_.

9. Paul isn't interested in politics. His friends aren't interested in politics.

   Paul isn't interested in politics, _and neither are his f_.

   Paul isn't interested in politics, _and his f aren't either_.

10. Michael decorates homes. Andrea decorates homes.

    Michael decorates homes, _and so does A._.

    Michael decorates homes, _and A does too_.

101 Clear Grammar Tests **TEST 66**

Part C Circle the letter of the answer that correctly completes each sentence.

1. Irene is going to college _____ a good job after she graduates.

   (A) for to get

   (B) so to get

   (C) in order to get

   (D) for get

2. Justin called his father _____ some career advice.

   (A) for

   (B) in order to

   (C) to

   (D) so

3. Andre always volunteers for special committees _____ a good reputation at work.

   (A) for earn

   (B) in order to earn

   (C) so to earn

   (D) for to earn

4. Oliver is lying on a beach towel, _____.

   (A) and neither is Sanford

   (B) and so Sanford is

   (C) and Sanford is too

   (D) and Sanford is either

5. Tucson has a lot of tourists in the winter, _____.

   (A) and Santa Fe does too

   (B) however so does Santa Fe

   (C) and Santa Fe has too

   (D) and so Santa Fe does

6. The two students were in different rooms during the test. _____, they could not have cheated.

   (A) Since

   (B) However

   (C) Therefore

   (D) In order to

7. Susan hasn't graduated yet, _____.

   (A) and either has Sarah

   (B) and neither has Sarah

   (C) and Sarah has neither

   (D) and neither did Sarah

8. Fred needs to earn more money, _____ he's going to ask his boss for a raise.

   (A) therefore

   (B) so

   (C) however

   (D) since

9. I need to buy something for dinner. _____, I don't have any money.

   (A) So

   (B) Therefore

   (C) However

   (D) Either

10. Ellen loves to go skiing, _____.

    (A) and so Gretchen does

    (B) and Gretchen does too

    (C) and Gretchen do too

    (D) and neither does Gretchen

101 Clear Grammar Tests **TEST 66**   150

VERB + Direct or Indirect Object

Clear Grammar 3, Unit 11

Name _____   Date _____

Part A Write *to me* or *for me* on the line.

1. She gave the book _____.

2. Kevin introduced Linda _____.

3. The teacher answered all of the questions _____.

4. The doctor prescribed this medicine _____.

5. Could you answer this question _____?

6. He said good-bye _____, and then he got on the plane.

7. Would you open the door _____? My hands are totally full.

8. The clerk showed the newest shoes _____.

9. Could you do a small favor _____?

10. Please bring these files back _____ when you are finished using them.

11. She's thinking about buying a new sweater _____ for my birthday.

12. The doctor explained the correct way to take this medicine _____.

Part B Look at the underlined parts in these sentences. If it is correct, circle C. If it is wrong, circle X, and write the correct form on the line. Three of the sentences are wrong.

C   X   1.   Before I boarded my flight back to the U.S., I <u>said good-bye to my host family members</u> who were at the airport to see me off.

_____

C   X   2.   Don't be shy about <u>asking me questions</u> during class.

_____

C   X   3.   Please <u>describe me your new car</u>.

_____

C   X   4.   My cousin was nice enough to <u>change his plans for me</u> so that I could use his car all day yesterday.

_____

Clear Grammar 3

C   X   5.   Mr. Williams plans to <u>buy dinner for all of us</u>.

_____

C   X   6.   I can't remember how much <u>this shirt cost to me</u>.

_____

C   X   7.   I'm so grateful to Jerry for <u>doing this favor for me</u>.

_____

C   X   8.   He didn't <u>tell to me the answers</u>.

_____

TEST 68 VERB + Direct or Indirect Object

Clear Grammar 3, Unit 11

Name _____   Date _____

Part A Circle the letters (a, b, or c) of the forms that are possible when you are expressing direct and indirect objects.

1. a. give me the book   b. give the book to me   c. give the book for me
2. a. explain me the word   b. explain the word to me   c. explain the word for me
3. a. say me "hello"   b. say hello to me   c. say "hello" for me
4. a. cost me $100   b. cost $100 to me   c. cost $100 for me
5. a. speak me English   b. speak English to me   c. speak English for me
6. a. give me it   b. give it to me   c. give it for me
7. a. make me a cake   b. make a cake to me   c. make a cake for me
8. a. find me a chair   b. find a chair to me   c. find a chair for me
9. a. wish me good luck   b. wish good luck to me   c. wish good luck for me
10. a. open me the door   b. open the door to me   c. open the door for me
11. a. do me a favor   b. do a favor to me   c. do a favor for me
12. a. make me it   b. make it to me   c. make it for me
13. a. introduce me him   b. introduce him to me   c. introduce him for me
14. a. bring me the cup   b. bring the cup to me   c. bring the cup for me
15. a. pass me the salt   b. pass the salt to me   c. pass the salt for me
16. a. explain me the word   b. explain the word to me   c. explain the word for me

Part B Write the one verb in the parentheses that can correctly complete each sentence.

1. (open, show, get)   I am going to _____ my new car to my

   cousin.

2. (asked, answered, explained) The teacher _____ the question to me.

3. (buy, wish, give)   We decided to _____ a watch to our niece.

4. (sent, saved, charged)   Mrs. Wilson _____ ten dollars to Joseph.

5. (open, pass, repeat)   Please _____ me the salt.

6. (open, pass, repeat)   Please _____ the salt to me.

7. (tells, says, pronounces)   Patricia always _____ "hello" to me.

8. (made, announced, said)   Our boss _____ the new schedule to everyone.

Clear Grammar 3, Units 2–11

Name _____ Date _____

Part A Phrasal verbs. Fill in the blanks with the correct word or definition. Follow the example.

Example: To fill ___*in*___ the blank means to write information in the blank.

To fill out means ___*to complete a paper or form*___.

1. To eat _____ means to eat at a restaurant.

2. To find out something means to _____.

3. If you can count on your friends, that means that you _____.

4. To call _____ something means to cancel it, but to put _____ something means to delay it.

5. To hurry _____ means to go faster.

6. To put something _____ means to wear it, and the opposite is to take it _____.

7. Look at how many phrasal verbs start with *look:* To look _____ means to look for information in a dictionary or on the Internet; to look _____ means to take care of someone or something; and to look _____ _____ something means to be careful.

8. If somebody says, "Please hold on," he or she means _____.

9. To pick _____ has two meanings: to lift or to go get someone.

10. To hand out something means _____.

Part B Underline the words that correctly complete each sentence.

❶ (Had you ever gone, Were you ever going, Have you ever gone) to Australia? We ❷ (had, were having, have had) a ❸ (great, greatly) vacation there last year. We ❹ (spent, were spending, have spent) a month traveling ❺ (by, with) helicopter, bus and four-wheel drive across the Northern Territory. In the Red Center of the Northern Territory, we were excited ❻ (of, for, about) seeing Uluru—that's Ayers Rock—and the nearby Kata Tjutu, ❼ (but, so, therefore) we decided ❽ (to take, taking) a helicopter tour of the area. While we ❾ (flew, were flying, have flown), we listened

⑩ (intent, intently) as our pilot Steve told us about the sights. He was very familiar **⑪** (to, with, about) the area's history and Aboriginal Dreamtime beliefs because he had grown up there. Later, we **⑫** (took, were taking, have taken) the bus north toward Darwin, in the lush top part of the Northern Territory. Near there we saw Kakadu National Park, **⑬** (who, which) **⑭** (made, was making, was made) famous to non-Australians by the movie *Crocodile Dundee*. In Kakadu, we saw Aborigine rock paintings **⑮** (who, which) **⑯** (estimate, are estimating, are estimated) by anthropologists to date from 20,000 years ago up to the 1960s. We also saw the spectacular Jim Jim Falls and Twin Falls, crocodiles and other wildlife, and a variety of flora. There is so much more to tell about our adventures in Australia's Northern Territory that I could go on and on. It was the vacation of a lifetime, and we plan **⑰** (to visit, visiting) Australia again **⑱** (for, because, in order to) see more of this amazing country. If you **⑲** (didn't go, weren't going, haven't been) there yet, I recommend **⑳** (to go, going)!

TEST 70 Review of Book 3

Clear Grammar 3, Units 2–11

Name _____ Date _____

Part A Read each sentence carefully. Look at the underlined part. If the underlined part is correct, circle C. If it is wrong, circle X, and write the correct answer on the line. Eight of the sentences are wrong.

C   X   1. It's dark in here! <u>Turn off</u> the light!

_____

C   X   2. Nina was watching TV <u>while her mother was cooking</u> dinner.

_____

C   X   3. <u>I've just finished</u> my homework, so I can go out now.

_____

C   X   4. Andrea studied for her medical terminology test <u>by writing</u> the terms and definitions on index cards.

_____

C   X   5. Every adult should <u>be responsible to</u> his or her own actions.

_____

C   X   6. New Year's Day <u>celebrated</u> on January 1st.

_____

C   X   7. Mr. Laxer is <u>the person who taught</u> me the most about life.

_____

C   X   8. The car <u>that we decided to buy</u> gets good gas mileage.

_____

C   X   9. This lecture is not at all interesting. I am very <u>boring</u>.

_____

C   X   10. I'm glad I <u>remembered to stop</u> at the store on my way home. I have no milk at all.

_____

C   X   11.   Tomas <u>wants visiting</u> Egypt in the coming year.

_____

C   X   12.   Catherine runs four miles every day <u>in order to stay</u> in good shape.

_____

C   X   13.   Marcos <u>repeated his request to</u> his boss.

_____

C   X   14.   Cutting coupons <u>saves me</u> about 20 percent every time I go shopping.

_____

C   X   15.   When the doorbell rang, I stopped <u>to talk</u> on the phone to see who

was there.

_____

C   X   16.   Jim wasn't home when I called him this morning, so I will <u>call him back</u>

later.

_____

C   X   17.   I didn't like vegetables when I was a little girl, but now <u>I'm liking</u> them

a lot.

_____

C   X   18.   This is the third time that I <u>have had to re-write</u> the same essay.

_____

C   X   19.   <u>Matthew wisely decided</u> to drop his lowest test score.

_____

C   X   20.   Gina is <u>happy in</u> have her boyfriend with her on her birthday.

_____

Part B Circle the letter of the answer that correctly completes each sentence.

1. Brad was so angry when he read the contract that he _____ into little pieces.

(A) tore up it   (C) torn it up

(B) tore it up   (D) torn up it

2. _____ my father, I hugged him.

(A) When I saw   (C) While I saw

(B) When I was seeing   (D) While I was seeing

Clear Grammar 3

3. So far this year, Nancy _____ over $1,000 to charity.

   (A) gave

   (B) given

   (C) has gave

   (D) has given

4. Maya _____, so she is easy to understand.

   (A) clearly speaks

   (B) clear speaks

   (C) speaks clearly

   (D) speaks clear

5. Does your mother _____ your going out alone at night?

   (A) approve for

   (B) approve on

   (C) approve to

   (D) approve of

6. The Statue of Liberty _____ by millions of people every year.

   (A) visits

   (B) visited

   (C) is visits

   (D) is visited

7. Lee Harvey Oswald appears to be _____ President Kennedy.

   (A) the person shot who

   (B) that person which shot

   (C) the person who shot

   (D) the person shot

8. _____ to classical music is very relaxing.

   (A) Listen

   (B) Listening

   (C) Listens

   (D) To listening

9. Sheila called her mother _____ some recipes from her.

   (A) to get

   (B) for to get

   (C) for get

   (D) in order for get

10. Elaine _____ her co-workers.

    (A) introduced her best friend

    (B) introduced her to best friend

    (C) introduced her best friend to

    (D) introduced to her

11. Jennie is deathly _____ spiders. She doesn't even like to think about them!

    (A) afraid to

    (B) afraid on

    (C) afraid of

    (D) afraid by

12. Before the plane _____, we _____ to fasten our seatbelts.

    (A) was departed . . . were told

    (B) departed . . . told

    (C) was departed . . . told

    (D) departed . . . were told

13. Venice is _____ my heart.

   (A) the city who stole   (C) the city that was stole

   (B) the city that stoles   (D) the city that stole

14. I'm very nervous right now. I don't remember _____ my stove before I left.

   (A) to turn off   (C) to turning off

   (B) turning off   (D) turn off

15. Jackie went to the store _____ some soda and chips.

   (A) for   (C) in order to

   (B) so   (D) to

Part C Underline the word or words that correctly complete each sentence.

1. We (ran out of, ran into) gas on our way to Sarasota, so we had to call a tow truck.

2. Before Juan came to the United States, he (didn't know, wasn't knowing) any English.

3. The choir (has sung, has sang) two songs so far this evening.

4. Kevin has worked (hardly, hard) to earn a good reputation in the publishing field.

5. Victor thanked his father (to, for) the help with his science project.

6. Marilyn Monroe (died, was died) in the 1960s.

7. I really admire the courage (that Tom has, who Tom has) to fight for his country.

8. Oscar wants his daughter (to call, to calls) him when she gets home from school.

9. Paul has a large house, and Chris (does, has) too.

10. The teacher pronounced the list of words (to, for) us.

11. We need to (put on, put out) the fire in the fireplace before we go to sleep.

12. (While, When) the movie started, the theater got quiet.

13. Rose (went, has gone) to the store twice so far this week.

14. Walter is a (fast, fastly) talker. It's usually hard to understand what he's saying.

15. What (was happened, happened) when you told your mother about your test score?

TEST 71 Past Perfect Tense

Clear Grammar 4, Unit 2

Name _____   Date _____

Part A Circle the letter of the answer that correctly completes each sentence.

1. The past perfect tense indicates past actions that occurred _____.

    (A) just a few minutes ago

    (B) before another past event, action or time

    (C) after another past even, action or time

2. The past perfect progressive tense indicates the duration of an event or that an event

    _____.

    (A) happened after another event, action, or time

    (B) had finished before another event, action, or time

    (C) was in progress before another event, action, or time

3. The contraction *she'd* in *She'd already spoken to him before I arrived* means _____.

    (A) she had

    (B) she did

    (C) she would

4. Do not use the past progressive form with _____.

    (A) action and nonaction verbs

    (B) action verbs and actions that are repeated a number of times

    (C) nonaction verbs and actions that are repeated a number of times

5. The past perfect contraction *it'd* is acceptable _____.

    (A) in spoken English only

    (B) in written English only

    (C) in neither spoken nor written English

Clear Grammar 4

Part B Combine the sentences using the word in parentheses. Change one of the verbs to past perfect or past perfect progressive in order to make the sentence correct. Follow the example.

Example: The children already finished their homework. (when) Their mom came home. *The children had already finished their homework when their mom came home.*

1. Manuel studied English for six years. (before) He started college in the U.S.

   _____

2. Lynn wasn't working at the company very long. (when) She was offered a promotion.

   _____

3. Shawn never experienced an earthquake. (until) She lived in Japan.

   _____

4. (before) William moved to Texas. He always lived in the Northwest.

   _____

5. They got engaged. (after) They were dating for just one month.

   _____

6. I was waiting for 35 minutes. (when) The receptionist told me that the doctor wouldn't be able to see me as scheduled.

   _____

7. Elizabeth was married and divorced twice. (before) She turned 24.

   _____

8. We didn't join Bob and Sara at the restaurant. (because) We already ate dinner at home.

   _____

9. The documents were hidden inside the wall for 100 years. (before) They were found in 1999.

   _____

10. Thomas and his friends finally reached New Orleans. (after) They were driving for 20 hours.

   _____

Clear Grammar 4, Unit 2

Name _____   Date _____

Part A   Fill in the blanks with the correct form of the verb in parentheses. Use either the past perfect or the simple past. Follow the example.

Ann: (become) ❶ _*Had*_ George Washington _*become*_ president before he (win)

❷ _____ his first battle?

Rob: No. He (win) ❸ _____ his first battle in 1781, and then he (become)

❹ _____ president in 1789.

Brett: (live) ❺ How long _____ Alexander Graham Bell _____

in Scotland before he (come) ❻ _____ to the United States?

Suzy: Well, he (be) ❼ _____ born in 1847, and he (come) ❽ _____ to the

United States in 1870, so he (live) ❾ _____ in Scotland for 13 years.

Chuck: (be) ❿ How long _____ the United States _____

a country before France (give) ⓫ _____ it the Statue of Liberty?

Lucy: The French (give) ⓬ _____ the statue to the United States to

commemorate its centennial, so the country (be) ⓭ _____ 100 years old.

Part B   Write these statements in the past perfect or past perfect progressive. Be sure to make a negative sentence if it is indicated. Follow the example.

Example: When I came home, I knew that my cat (feeling well [neg]).

   When I came home, I knew that my cat hadn't been feeling well.

1. When Dan got to the office, he knew that the boss (looking) for him for a while.

   _____

2. Gina was thrilled to see her boyfriend because she (see [neg]) him for two weeks.

   _____

3. Alex (find) two seashells before his mother told him to put them down.

   _____

4. Elaine and Diane (shopping) for six hours before they found the perfect prom dresses.

   _____

5. Marsha went to the doctor because she (eat [neg]) anything for two days.

_____

6. Monica (be) to Europe two times before she went there for her wedding.

_____

7. The young couple didn't realize that they (dancing) for hours.

_____

8. Noreen didn't want to go to sleep because she (finished [neg]) the quilt she was

working on.

_____

9. Georgette (working) in customer service for 11 years when she was finally promoted to

manager.

_____

10. The pot of water boiled over because I (watching [neg]) it.

_____

Part C Read each sentence carefully. Look at the underlined part. If the underlined part is correct, circle C. If the underlined part is wrong, circle X, and write the correct answer on the line. Six of the sentences are wrong.

C X 1. How long had you been studying English when you left your country?

_____

C X 2. What universities had you consider before you chose this one?

_____

C X 3. Sam had been working at the motorcycle shop for 10 years before he quit

and returned to school.

_____

C X 4. How long the party had been going on when you arrived?

_____

C X 5. Had you been waiting long when you were finally allowed into the

theme park?

_____

C X 6. Before this last meteor shower, there hadn't been being a meteor shower

in 75 years.

_____

C　X　7.　Jan <u>had been running</u> for 20 minutes when she tripped and hurt her ____ ankle.

_____

C　X　8.　Mike <u>hadn't prepare</u> for the test, so he failed it.

_____

C　X　9.　Debbie <u>had teaching</u> at the university for 8 years when she was offered a permanent position.

_____

C　X　10.　<u>You had known</u> your girlfriend long before you asked her to marry you?

_____

Clear Grammar 4, Unit 3

Name _____   Date _____

Part A Look at the suffixes in the box. Are they used to form verbs, adjectives, or nouns? Write them on the lines in the correct category, and then give an example for each.

Example: **ADJECTIVES**

-ive expensive

-ize	-ish	-less	-ist	-ship
-ful	-tion	-able/-ible	-ness	-er/-or/-ar
-ify	-ment	-en	-ous	-an/-ian/-ean

VERBS	**ADJECTIVES**	**NOUNS**
_____	_____	_____
_____	_____	_____
_____	_____	_____
	_____	_____
	_____	_____
		_____
		_____

Part B Write the correct word form in the blank. Do not use the same word form twice.

1. If you behave _____ toward people, they might be _____ to you too.
   (rude, rudely, rudeness)

2. Shuiling plays the violin _____. Her music is exceptionally _____.
   (beauty, beautify, beautiful, beautifully)

3. An _____ is a highly creative person. Are you _____? (art, artist, artistic, artistically)

4. Do you know how to _____ this word? You can find the _____ in the dictionary. (pronounce, pronounceable, pronunciation)

5. Olympic athletes have _____ strength, talent, and determination. Watching them train for the Sydney Olympics left a lasting _____ on me. (impress, impressive, impressively, impression)

6. Some people say that money cannot buy _____. If they give me the money, I will _____ try it out to see if it's true or not. (happy, happily, happiness)

7. Neurosurgeons must have great _____. They use special tools to help them perform these surgeries as _____ as possible. (accurate, accurately, accuracy)

8. Dogs are said to be man's best friend because they are so _____. They obey their master's orders _____. (faith, faithful, faithfully, faithfulness)

9. Drinking and driving is very _____ . You put yourself, your passengers, and other drivers in _____ when you drink and drive. (danger, dangerous, dangerously)

10. Could you please _____ me? You are such a _____ person. (help, helpful, helpfully, helpfulness)

11. Is Helen _____? No, she's British, but she's lived here for 20 years, so she has become quite _____. (America, American, Americanized)

12. The doctors were able to _____ Mr. Green's heart rate and blood pressure, so his condition is now _____. (stable, stability, stabilize, stabilized)

13. Do you have any _____ in astronomy? I have two tickets to the science center and planetarium, and I've heard that its new show is _____. Would you like to go? (interest, interesting, interested, interestingly)

14. Sandee has been my _____ since we were in middle school. Our _____ has lasted for 25 years. (friend, friendly, friendliness, friendship)

15. Viviana has been a very _____ graphic designer for 10 years. Now she plans to start her own graphics business, and she hopes it will _____. (succeed, success, successful, successfully)

Clear Grammar 4, Unit 3

Name _____ Date _____

Part A Underline the word form that correctly completes each sentence.

1. It is important to (hydrify, hydrate) your body before, during, and after exercising.

2. To help you (lessate, lessen) your work load, I'll help you with some of your projects.

3. During the debate, the candidate (minimated, minimized) his role in voting against allotting funds for education.

4. The young couple (solidicated, solidified) their relationship by getting engaged.

5. Kim was (nervy, nervous) when she sat down to take the comprehensive exam.

6. Sam is my most (dependable, dependal) friend. I can always count on him.

7. Chewing (sugarless, sugarful) gum can help diminish your cravings for sweets.

8. The doctor referred to his (medicament, medical) dictionary for help with diagnosing a patient.

9. The (elusish, elusive) bank robber had successfully robbed six banks in the local area.

10. Freida asked her financial (consulted, consultant) for advice on her retirement account.

Part B Circle the letter of the answer that correctly completes each sentence.

1. The 5-year-old boy is _____ and won't share his toys with anyone.

   (A) selfate   (C) selfish

   (B) selfous   (D) selfy

2. Arnold wants to visit the _____ country of Ghana after he gets out of college.

   (A) African   (C) Africa

   (B) Africish   (D) Africal

3. After years of _____ insults and arguments, the couple decided to divorce.

   (A) hurtful   (C) hurtless

   (B) hurtable   (D) hurtified

4. Luisa spoke _____ to her sleeping baby.

   (A) quietful   (C) quietly

   (B) quietate   (D) quietic

5. To the employees' surprise, there was a sudden _____ of the management's decision.

   (A) reversive   (C) reversal

   (B) reverism   (D) reverseship

6. To have a solid _____, communication is a _____.

   (A) relationship . . . necessitate   (C) realtionity . . . necessary

   (B) realtionate . . . necessary   (D) relationship . . . necessity

7. The United States celebrates its _____ on July 4th.

   (A) independent   (C) independence

   (B) independity   (D) independment

8. Because of his genuine _____ for his best friend, Juan offered to lend him money to help him out of his predicament.

   (A) fondness   (C) fondship

   (B) fondity   (D) fondant

9. David took his pants to the _____ to have them shortened.

   (A) tailist   (C) tailure

   (B) tailor   (D) tailar

10. The _____ at the _____office wrote down my name and appointment time.

    (A) receptionist . . . doctor's   (C) receptionist . . . docter's

    (B) receptioner . . . doctor's   (D) receptioner . . . docter's

Part C Read the underlined parts. If the part is correct, circle C. If the part is wrong, circle X, and write the correct answer on the line. Six of the sentences are wrong.

C X 1. The <u>failment</u> of the committee to act in a timely manner resulted in the workers' going on strike. _____

C X 2. The doctor gave the <u>elderly</u> man a prescription for pain medication.

_____

C X 3. Our mother said she wouldn't allow the <u>foolishness</u> to continue, and she made us climb down from the tree. _____

C X 4. As a result of his unemployment, Roger faced months of financial <u>hardly</u>.

_____

C X 5. <u>Communism and capitalism</u> are mutually exclusive.

_____

C X 6. Everyone seemed to enjoy the <u>frivolment</u> of the evening's events.

_____

C X 7. Although the sky had been clear, it <u>suddenish</u> started to rain.

_____

C X 8. Garbage collectors are an <u>indispensable</u> part of society.

_____

C X 9. The soldier's <u>heroific</u> actions earned him a military honor.

_____

C X 10. Being a <u>considerful</u> person, Gene was careful not to serve pork to his Muslim guests. _____

TEST 75 Conditionals: *If* Clauses and *Wish*

Clear Grammar 4, Unit 4

Name _____   Date _____

Part A Read each sentence, and look at the underlined verbs. If the verb is correct, circle C. If it is wrong, circle X, and write the correction on the line. Seven sentences are wrong.

C   X   1.   If I <u>win</u> the lottery, I would buy a yacht and sail around the world.

_____

C   X   2.   If Native Americans <u>hadn't introduced</u> Europeans to chocolate, we

wouldn't have chocolate candy bars today. _____

C   X   3.   I would call the doctor if I <u>were</u> you. _____

C   X   4.   She will trade in her old car if the credit union <u>approves</u> her loan

application for a new car. _____

C   X   5.   I wish I <u>would of studied</u> more for the exam. _____

C   X   6.   Most Americans believe that if you <u>will work</u> hard, you can succeed at

almost anything. _____

C   X   7.   David wishes he <u>could have met</u> his paternal grandfather before he died.

_____

C   X   8.   Gina realized that if she <u>had been paying</u> attention, she wouldn't have

run the red light. _____

C   X   9.   If you <u>preferred</u> warm sunny weather, you probably won't like London.

_____

C   X   10.   Do you wish you <u>had</u> the ability to see the future? _____

C   X   11.   If I <u>finish</u> work in time, I will stop at the bank on the way home.

_____

C   X   12.   I wish I <u>can understand</u> Portuguese because I love bossa nova music.

_____

C   X   13. <u>Were</u> the first American immigrants alive today, they would be very surprised at how much the United States has changed. _____

C   X   14. Could you please call me if you <u>found</u> the information? _____

C   X   15. If English <u>was</u> easier, I would be able to speak it fluently. _____

Part B Look at the following real and unreal/unlikely situations. Write a sentence for each. Use an *if* clause in each sentence and watch your verbs. Follow the example.

    Example: have a flat tire   <u>*If I had a flat tire, I would put on the spare and drive home.*</u>

  1. win a million dollars

    _____

  2. don't understand something

    _____

  3. have a headache

    _____

  4. see a cockroach in my house

    _____

  5. meet Brad Pitt

    _____

Part C Write three sentences expressing your wishes.

  1. _____

  2. _____

  3. _____

TEST 76 Conditionals: *If* Clauses and *Wish*

Clear Grammar 4, Unit 4

Name _____   Date _____

Part A Fill in the blanks with the correct form of the verb to make unreal conditions in the present and future. Follow the example.

  Example: If I ___*were*___ (be) younger, I ___*would be*___ (be) in better physical shape.

1. If any of us _____ (know) how to start a fire, we _____ (be) a lot warmer right now.

2. If we _____ (need) help, we _____ (light) these flares to attract attention.

3. If you really _____ (want) to pass this class, you _____ (study) more regularly.

4. If I _____ (speak) Italian, I _____ (try) to get a job in Italy.

5. If Dan _____ (ask) for help with his bills, his roommate _____ (lend) him some money.

6. You _____ (run) farther distances if you _____ (train) harder.

7. If you _____ (complete) all your assignments on time, you _____ (be) promoted to manager.

8. If you _____ (see) things from my perspective, you _____ (disagree, not) with me.

9. If I _____ (be) you, I _____ (try) to get more rest each day.

10. *Tim:* Can you help me translate this letter from Spanish into English?

    Sue: Of course, I _____ (help) you with that letter, if my Spanish _____ _____ (be) better.

Part B Underline the verb form that correctly completes each sentence. Follow the example.

Example: If the room is too cold, my fingers (*get*, got) numb.

1. If the hurricane heads this way, they (will close, closed) some of the roads.

2. If you (went, go) to Switzerland, you should visit Bern.

3. If I had more money, I (bought, would buy) a reliable car.

4. If Andy had stayed in the Air Force, he (will be, would have been) an officer by now.

5. If you hadn't been home when I called, I don't know what I (would have done, will do).

6. I wish there (was, were) a way to be fully rested after only a 30-minute nap.

7. English wouldn't be so confusing if you (had, have) more experience with it.

8. If we (go, went) to the beach, we can get some much needed sun.

9. If it doesn't rain tomorrow, we (will have, would have) a picnic in the park.

10. Had you asked me, I (will help, would have helped) you.

Part C Circle the letter of the answer that correctly completes each sentence.

1. If I _____ this test, I _____ a big dinner to celebrate.

   (A) pass . . . will have   (C) pass . . . would have

   (B) passed . . . will have   (D) passed . . . had

2. If you _____ me when you get home, I _____ worried.

   (A) didn't call . . . will be   (C) don't call . . . will be

   (B) don't call . . . would be   (D) didn't call . . . am

3. _____ around the world if you retire early?

   (A) Will travel   (C) You will travel

   (B) Will you travel   (D) Did you travel

4. If you _____ a passport, you _____ the country.

   (A) didn't have . . . can't leave   (C) don't have . . . couldn't leave

   (B) didn't have . . . don't leave   (D) don't have . . . can't leave

5. If I _____ how to dance, I _____ every weekend.

   (A) know . . . could have gone out   (C) knew . . . can go out

   (B) knew . . . could go out   (D) know . . . could go out

6. Fred _____ a lot of money if he _____ more careful each week.

   (A) could have saved . . . had been (C) could save . . . have been

   (B) can save . . . would have been (D) can saved . . . had been

7. If you _____, maybe I could understand what you're saying.

   (A) aren't screaming (C) weren't screaming

   (B) didn't screaming (D) don't screaming

8. I wish you _____ to help out around the house.

   (A) try (C) have tried

   (B) would try (D) are trying

9. Don't you wish we _____ from school tomorrow?

   (A) can stay home (C) could stay home

   (B) will stay home (D) stay home

10. If you _____ your balance, you might have overdrawn your account.

    (A) had checked (C) check

    (B) didn't check (D) hadn't checked

TEST 77 Adverb Clauses

Clear Grammar 4, Unit 5

Name _____   Date _____

Part A Look at the clauses in the box. Some are dependent adverb clauses, and some are independent clauses. Combine one clause from Column A with one clause from Column B to make a logical sentence. Write that sentence on the lines below the box, using a capital letter and a period. Add a comma to the sentence if needed.

COLUMN A	COLUMN B
he is such a popular singer that	she studies for one hour
please call me	if I won the lottery
whether they want to or not	we still receive calls from telemarketers
you can find friends	many people want to be bilingual
since Sam was a young boy	if she eats food containing peanuts
Georgina has a severe allergic reaction	my sister is going to take care of our house
I would buy a house in the Greek Islands	as soon as you get this message
while we are on vacation in Hawaii	people wait in line all day to buy a concert ticket
before Ling comes to school in the morning	I like to spend quiet evenings at home
though we registered on the do-not-call list	all workers must pay federal income tax
whereas my husband prefers to go out	he has always loved taking care of animals
so that they will have better job opportunities	wherever you go in the world

1. _____

2. _____

3. _____

4. _____

5. _____

6. _____

7. _____

8. _____

9. _____

10. _____

11. _____

12. _____

Part B Read the sentences, and underline the correct adverb clause connector.

1. We must conserve the world's natural resources (as, as if, as though) conservationists have recommended.

2. (If, Unless, Whether or not) we don't, future generations will face the consequences.

3. Many basketball players are (so, such, such a) tall that they must have all their clothes custom-made.

4. If an earthquake hits, you should get under a table or stand in a doorway or other pro- tected location and stay there (when, until, as soon as) the earthquake stops.

5. The Golden Triangle is the area (where, wherever, anywhere) the borders of Thailand, Myanmar, and Laos meet.

6. My cousin usually makes (so, such, such a) spicy food that I cannot eat it!

7. I told him he needs to make it less spicy (since, in that, so that) I can enjoy my meal.

8. (So, After, Until) the doctor checked the test results, she told me that I was in perfect health.

9. Although the use of credit cards is becoming commonplace, you still cannot use them (where, anywhere, everywhere) in the world.

10. (As though, Even though, Because) he has $10,000 in credit card debt, my brother won't stop using his credit cards.

11. (While, when, because) Millie hasn't traveled outside of the U.S., her sister has lived all around the world.

12. Jeong-hee is looking forward to December (even though, while, because) she is going to graduate with her master's degree.

TEST 78 Adverb Clauses

Clear Grammar 4, Unit 5

Name _____   Date _____

Part A Underline the connectors that correctly complete each sentence.

1. (After, Until) the wedding ceremony ended, there was a huge party in a fancy hotel.

2. (By the time that, When) my mother gets home, she cooks dinner.

3. Annie brought an umbrella with her (because, so that) it was going to rain.

4. (Since, So that) his house increased in value, Kevin sold it for a profit.

5. (Because, Although) the candidate campaigned vigorously, he lost the election.

6. (If, While) red meat is not very healthful, fish and lean meats are.

7. We will meet on Sunday to review our homework (unless, given that) we haven't finished by then.

8. Liverpool, England, is the city (anywhere, where) the Beatles originated.

9. Our teacher spoke (in order that, as if) we were not going to have an exam.

10. (As soon as, By the time that) you get this letter, please let me know.

Part B Circle the letter of the answer that correctly completes each sentence.

1. _____ I got out of bed, I knew I was too sick to go to work.

   (A) If   (C) Once

   (B) Since   (D) Till

2. Our family has lived in New York _____ I can remember.

   (A) as long as   (C) in the event that

   (B) despite the fact that   (D) inasmuch as

3. The little girls stayed awake _____ the sun rose.

   (A) even though   (C) till

   (B) provided that   (D) whereas

4. The men were watching a football game _____ the women were preparing dinner.

   (A) if   (C) where

   (B) while   (D) so that

5. _____ my car broke down, I wasn't able to get to work on time.

   (A) Even though   (C) Unless

   (B) Since   (D) So that

6. _____ his check had been deposited, Noel was able to pay some of his bills.

   (A) Though   (C) Despite the fact that

   (B) In case   (D) Given that

7. _____ he is afraid of flying, Roger joined the Air Force.

   (A) In the event that   (C) Only if

   (B) As long as   (D) Despite the fact that

8. _____ Los Angeles has a lively nightlife, San Francisco is more laid-back.

   (A) If   (C) In case

   (B) When   (D) Whereas

9. Luis promised to support his children _____ they chose to go to college.

   (A) so that   (C) whether or not

   (B) whereas   (D) everywhere

10. _____ the flight is cancelled, we will probably take a train.

   (A) Even though   (C) So that

   (B) In the event that   (D) Until

Part C Read each sentence carefully. Look at the underlined part. If the underlined part is correct, circle C. If the underlined part is wrong, circle X, and write the correct answer on the line. Five of the sentences are wrong.

C   X   1. When the waitress <u>will comes</u> to our table, please tell her I'd like

            the chicken. _____

C   X   2. <u>Until I finished</u> reading the novel, I didn't have a clue that the police

            officer committed the crimes. _____

C   X   3. <u>By time</u> the football game ended, half the people had left the stadium.

            _____

C   X   4. Now that everyone is here, we <u>can't</u> begin the meeting. _____

C   X   5. <u>Although</u> she is a lazy person, Gina runs three miles a day to stay

            in shape. _____

C   X   6. Though we saved money to go on vacation, <u>but we didn't have enough</u> to cover the whole trip. _____

C   X   7. <u>Provided that</u> you finish your homework early, we can go get some ice cream._____

C   X   8. <u>Despite of the fact that</u> it was his birthday, Tom still had to work a full day. _____

C   X   9. I will help you write your resume <u>only if</u> you make some effort to do it yourself. _____

C   X   10. There was <u>such a beautiful rainbow in the sky that</u> I had to pull over and look at it. _____

Clear Grammar 4, Unit 6

Name _____   Date _____

Part A Circle the letter of the answer that correctly completes each sentence.

1. Could you tell me _____ the international foods aisle?

   (A) where I found   (C) where I can find

   (B) where can I find   (D) where can be found

2. We have to hurry. The airline requires _____ there 90 minutes before our flight.

   (A) that we be   (C) that we are being

   (B) that we are   (D) that we will be

3. Linguists estimate _____ 40 percent or more of the world's languages may disappear over the next 50 to 100 years.

   (A) what   (C) than

   (B) that   (D) it

4. I wonder _____ Marcus will be at the waterfront conservation meeting tonight.

   (A) is   (C) if or not

   (B) that   (D) whether

5. Randy to Helena: "I'll call you on the weekend."

   Helena, talking to her friend two weeks later: "He said that __*B*__, but he didn't!"

   (A) he will call   (C) I'll call

   (B) he would call   (D) I would call

6. When Katrina arrived home three hours late, her worried mother asked her where _____.

   (A) was she   (C) had she been

   (B) she was   (D) she had been

7. _____ is a known fact today, but it was considered a dangerous lie when it was proposed.

   (A) The earth is round   (C) That the earth is round

   (B) The earth being round (D) Knowing that the earth is round

Part B Match each clause on the left with a noun clause on the right. Choose the most appropriate answer for each, and use each letter only once. Write the letter in the blank.

1. _____ Excuse me. Do you know

2. _____ Professor Gilliam recommended

3. _____ I would like to know

4. _____ The African farmers were relieved

5. _____ Investigators are still not sure

6. _____ Judging by the candidates, it seems

7. _____ Our insurance company told us

8. _____ I believe it is true

a. that we start our research as soon as possible.

b. when the rainy season finally started.

c. that this will be an interesting election year.

d. what time the meeting started?

e. that money cannot buy happiness.

f. how the fire began.

g. that our rates would go up because of the accident.

h. how many Aborigine tribes there are in Australia.

TEST 80   Noun Clauses

Clear Grammar 4, Unit 6

Name _____   Date _____

Part A   Underline the word or words that correctly complete each sentence.

1. Brett forgot (where, when) his wife is coming home.

2. Chris doesn't know (whether, if) or not he'll be able to play tennis with us.

3. Did you notice (what, that) the restaurant on the corner is being shut down?

4. I wonder (when, where) my cat is hiding.

5. Ask the attendant (where we can, where can we) park.

6. Tell me (how I can, how can I) help you work through your problems.

7. Can you tell me (where is the bank, where the bank is)?

8. It is encouraging (that, what) gas prices are beginning to decrease.

9. (Who, How) Frank won the race is a mystery to us all.

10. (Who, That) you learn from your mistakes is all that really matters.

11. The counselor advised me to (use, uses) additional resources.

12. Our teacher suggested that we (study, studies) thoroughly.

13. It is essential that you (are, be) at the lifeboat station when the bell rings.

14. Katie (told, said) me that her birthday is next week.

15. When I asked my father what he ate for dinner, he said he (eats, had eaten) steak.

Part B   Use the sentences to create noun clauses. The subject, verb, and tense for the main clause are in parentheses. Follow the example.

Example: Dogs are friendlier than cats. (Most people / agree [present])

_____*Most people agree that dogs are friendlier than cats.*_____

1. Men are complicated people. (Women / understand [present])

   _____

2. We can go to the park on Sunday. (Our father / promise [simple past])

   _____

3. Lake Okeechobee is the largest lake in Florida. (Our class / learn [simple past])

   _____

Clear Grammar 4

4. It is going to rain this weekend. (The weather map / indicate [simple present])

_____

5. She was late because she had car trouble. (We / guess [simple past])

_____

6. Knowledge of mathematics will benefit us. (The teacher / explain [simple past])

_____

7. A cure for cancer is possible. (Scientists / demonstrate [present perfect])

_____

8. He was in the area at the time of the crime. (The defendant / deny [simple present])

_____

9. Teen drug use is decreasing. (Studies / show [simple present])

_____

10. He was not home when the fire started. (The homeowner / claim [simple present])

_____

Part C Circle the letter of the answer that correctly completes each sentence.

1. Scientists discovered _____.

   (A) that the earth is round   (C) what the earth is round

   (B) where the earth is round   (D) when the earth is round

2. Do you know _____?

   (A) when school does let out   (C) when does school let out

   (B) when school let out   (D) when school lets out

3. I didn't understand _____, so I raised my hand.

   (A) what did my teacher said   (C) what did my teacher say

   (B) what my teacher did say   (D) what my teacher said

4. Do you know _____ outside?

   (A) why do we have to stand   (C) why we have to stand

   (B) where do we have stand   (D) why have we to stand

5. I can't remember _____.

   (A) who are those people   (C) who were those people

   (B) who those people are   (D) where were those people

6. The kids are excited _____ summer vacation begins next week.

   (A) what (C) that

   (B) when (D) where

7. Kelly is convinced _____ is going to quit his job.

   (A) that her husband (C) what her husband

   (B) whether her husband (D) her husband that

8. Bernard is relieved _____ is successful.

   (A) that is his restaurant (C) that is restaurant

   (B) that is restaurants (D) that his restaurant is

9. Linda was surprised _____ all her friends came to the party.

   (A) what (C) where

   (B) that (D) if

10. It is not known if _____.

   (A) are the astronauts safe (C) the astronauts safe

   (B) the astronauts are safe (D) are safe the astronauts

11. _____ the personal spacecraft landed safely is incredible news.

   (A) If (C) Whether

   (B) The fact that (D) What

12. I spoke to the doctor, and he said it is urgent that I _____ to the hospital.

   (A) am going (C) goes

   (B) went (D) go

13. John F. Kennedy said that we should ask _____ for our country.

   (A) what we can to do (C) what can we do

   (B) what we can did (D) what we can do

14. Nancy told me _____ she is going to Mexico for three weeks.

   (A) where (C) what

   (B) when (D) that

15. Jorge wanted to know _____ available to play tennis.

   (A) whether I was (C) whether am I

   (B) when was I (D) where I was

Clear Grammar 4, Unit 7

Name _____   Date _____

Part A Look at the sentences. The adjective or adverb clauses are underlined. Rewrite the sentence using a reduced clause. Follow the example.

Example: The attraction <u>that is most frequently visited in Florida</u> is Disney World.

    The attraction most frequently visited in Florida is Disney World.

1. People <u>who plan to move to Florida</u> usually do so because of the mild climate.

   _____

   _____

2. <u>While I was driving through the Ocala National Forest</u>, I saw a bear.

   _____

   _____

3. Runes, <u>which are a form of writing used in ancient times</u>, are often associated with magic and mystery.

   _____

   _____

4. <u>After they robbed Mrs. Grant's house</u>, the two men stole her car and led the police on a high-speed chase.

   _____

   _____

5. The car <u>that was stolen last night</u> was a black 2004 Ford Explorer with tinted windows.

   _____

   _____

6. For the party, let's use the crystal goblets <u>that are on the top shelf</u>.

   _____

   _____

7. They didn't enjoy their summertime visit to the Florida Keys <u>because it was too hot and humid</u>.

   _____

   _____

8. The salesperson <u>who earns the most in commissions this month</u> will get a bonus.

_____

_____

9. <u>Even though he was an hour late</u>, Eric expected his date to be there waiting for him.

_____

_____

10. The Statue of Liberty, <u>which is located in New York Harbor</u>, was a welcoming sight to the immigrants who arrived by ship in the early 1900s.

_____

_____

Part B Complete these sentences by putting an appositive after the subject with the correct punctuation and then adding an appropriate verb phrase. Follow the example.

Example: The computer, *the most important invention in recent years, has influenced how we communicate and how we study.*

1. Jackie Chan

_____

_____

2. The pyramids

_____

_____

3. Russia

_____

_____

4. English

_____

_____

5. Soccer

_____

_____

TEST 82　Reduction of Clauses

Clear Grammar 4, Unit 7

Name _____　　Date _____

Part A Read the following sentences, paying special attention to the underlined adjective clauses. Rewrite the sentences using adjective phrases that are reduced from adjective clauses. Follow the example.

Example: The cat <u>that is in the tree</u> is huge. ___*The cat in the tree is huge.*___

1. The dress <u>that is in the store window</u> is expensive.

   _____

2. The reporter <u>who is on TV right now</u> is a veteran.

   _____

3. The sofa <u>which is in our living room</u> needs to be replaced.

   _____

4. The astronaut <u>who is famous for being the first man on the moon</u> is Neil Armstrong.

   _____

5. Bill Gates, <u>who is one of the founders of Microsoft</u>, is extraordinarily wealthy.

   _____

6. Sorrento, <u>which is the town where my grandfather was born</u>, is in southern Italy.

   _____

7. The car <u>that was damaged in the accident</u> is still on the side of the road.

   _____

8. The person <u>who is elected president</u> has huge responsibilities.

   _____

9. The cake <u>that is sitting on the counter</u> is for tonight's dinner guests.

   _____

10. The people <u>who run the bakery</u> have decided to close the shop on Sundays.

   _____

Part B Read each sentence carefully. Look at the underlined part. If the underlined part is correct, circle C. If the underlined part is wrong, circle X, and write the correct form on the line. Five of the sentences are wrong.

C X 1. The teachers <u>were at the meeting</u> agreed to a new attendance policy.

_____

C X 2. Brie, <u>is a soft</u>, creamy cheese, is delicious on toasted bread.

_____

C X 3. The Statue of Liberty, <u>was built in 1886</u>, was a gift from France to the United States.

_____

C X 4. <u>After the examination</u>, the veterinarian told me my dog was fine.

_____

C X 5. <u>When the policeman stopped me</u>, he told me I had a broken taillight.

_____

C X 6. <u>Because being hungry</u>, John made a sandwich for himself.

_____

C X 7. <u>On account of her poor attendance</u>, Michelle was dismissed from school.

_____

C X 8. <u>The people responsible for the survey</u> collected valuable data.

_____

C X 9. <u>Hoping to save a lot of money</u> quickly, Gene got two jobs and stopped buying unnecessary things.

_____

C X 10. We have an insurance policy for <u>everything is worth $500</u> or more.

_____

Part C Read the following sentences, paying special attention to the underlined adverb clauses. Rewrite the sentences using adverb phrases that are reduced from adverb clauses. Follow the example.

Example: <u>When I am in town</u>, I spend time with my family.

When in town, I spend time with my family.

1. <u>While she is attending college</u>, Kim is holding down a full-time job.

_____

2. <u>When I am tired</u>, I find that I can't concentrate on anything.

_____

3. <u>While she was studying for her test</u>, Cindy realized that she had left out some material.

_____

4. <u>After he was robbed</u>, Don had to file a police report.

_____

5. <u>After she found her luggage</u>, Edna walked toward the airport parking lot.

_____

6. <u>When you are in trouble</u>, dial 9-1-1.

_____

7. <u>When she is confused about a grammar point</u>, Janet asks her teacher for help.

_____

8. <u>While he is eating</u>, my dog will snap at anyone who approaches him.

_____

9. <u>When I was notified about jury duty</u>, I reported to the courthouse to sign up.

_____

10. <u>When you are at the beach</u>, you should use plenty of sunscreen.

_____

Name _____   Date _____

Part A Fill in the blanks in the sentences with the appropriate affirmative or negative of these past modals: *may have*, *might have*, *must have*, *could have*, *would have*, or *should have*.

1. *Frank:*   You _shouldn't have_ taken the car to the mechanic for the oil change. I _could have_ done it myself.

   Anna: That's what you say, but you _would have_ procrastinated about it for weeks. It was faster and easier to take it to the mechanic.

2. *Domingo:*   Where do you think they are? It's 8:50 already, and we _should have_ been at the airport 20 minutes ago.

   Linda: They _may have_ had car trouble, but I think they _would have_ _could have_ called.

3. *Luz:*   Wow! Look at these animal tracks. What do you think _might have_ made them?

   Jean Robert: It _couldn't have_ been a dog; they're too big. It _must have_ been a wolf.

4. *Katrina:*   Look at all these bills! I _should have_ gone to law school and become a lawyer instead of a kindergarten teacher. I _would have_ made a lot more money.

   Lindsey: Yeah, but you _wouldn't have_ been as happy as you are teaching. You love your job!

Part B Read each sentence. Circle the correct modal, *could* or *be able to*. If both are possible, circle both.

1. I saw on the news today that a Dallas woman wrecked her car and was trapped in the burning wreckage, but the police officers (could/<u>were able to</u>) free her in time.

2. Until Yanos took lessons last year at the YMCA, he (couldn't/wasn't able to) swim.

3. I'm proud of my sister. She said she was going to run her first marathon and she (could/was able to) do it!

4. When Lori was younger, she (could/was able to) stand on her head, walk on her hands, do backbends, and do cartwheels. Now she doesn't have the flexibility.

5. Simphon went to traffic court to dispute a speeding ticket and (could, was able to) have it cancelled.

Part C Read the story, and fill in the blanks with the affirmative or negative of *would* or *used to* and the correct form of the verb in parentheses.

My younger sister and I are great friends now, but we didn't ❶ _____ (be) such good friends. That's because I ❷ _____ (play) mean jokes on her when we were little. I ❸ _____ (hide) in her closet before she went to bed at night, and then after about ten minutes had passed, I ❹ _____ (open) the closet door slowly, creeeaaaaak, like a monster in the closet! At that point, she ❺ _____ (yell), "Mom!" I also ❻ _____ (sneak) into her room while she was sleeping in the morning and draw freckles on her face with a colorful marker. Then, when she woke up and came to the breakfast table, I ❼ _____ (laugh) so hard until she figured out that I must have played another practical joke on her. These are just two of the many ways I ❽ _____ (torture) my cute little sister, who must have hated those jokes!

Part D Write sentences to answer the questions. Use past modals *had to*, *didn't have to*, *be supposed to*, or *be going to*.

1. a. What are some household chores or jobs you were obligated to do when you were growing up? b. What were some activities that you weren't obligated to do?

   a. _____

   _____

   b. _____

   _____

2. What were you planning or intending to do last weekend that you didn't get to do?

   _____

   _____

3. What was something you expected to do and were looking forward to but didn't do?

   _____

   _____

TEST 84 Past Modals

Clear Grammar 4, Unit 8

Name _____ Date _____

Part A Match each statement in the first column with the correct conclusion or obligation in the second column.

1. __d__ I didn't have time to call you last night.

    a. All the lights in the neighborhod are out.

2. __f__ Did you have to fix any windows after the storm?

    b. She must have forgotten about the test.

3. __b__ Our mother isn't home from work yet.

    c. It made all the windows shake.

4. __a__ Lightning had to have struck an electrical box.

    d. I had to study for an exam.

5. __h__ There was no electricity in the old days.

    e. He must not have heard the weather report.

6. __i__ I'm surprised Tomo isn't here yet.

    f. No. There was very little damage.

7. __j__ My cat was sick when I got home.

    g. You look very tired.

8. __e__ Tom is going sailing today.

    h. They had to use candles for light.

9. __c__ You had to have heard the noise.

    i. She must have had to stop at the store.

10. __g__ You must not have gotten much sleep.

    j. I had to take her to the vet.

Part B Circle the letter of the answer that correctly completes each sentence.

1. All the patio furniture is wet. _____ last night.

   (A) It may have rained   (C) It must have rained

   (B) It should have rained   (D) It may rained

2. I'm not sure where my neighbors are. They _____ out of town.

   (A) must be   (C) are

   (B) should be   (D) may be

3. Yesterday Gary _____ all his assignments.

   (A) could complete   (C) could be able to complete

   (B) was able to complete   (D) would have completed

4. This morning I _____ early enough to catch the bus.

   (A) could have got   (C) might have gotten

   (B) would have gotten out of bed   (D) couldn't get out of bed

5. Veronica _____ at the Sorbonne, but she decided to go to Oxford.

   (A) could have studied   (C) studied

   (B) had to have studied   (D) must have studied

6. When I was a little girl, my father _____ me around the house on his back.

   (A) had to carry   (C) would carry

   (B) must have carried   (D) would have carried

7. If I had known that you were low on cash, I _____ to lend you some money.

   (A) ought to have offered   (C) must have offered

   (B) was supposed to offered   (D) would have offered

8. You _____ called me when you got bored Saturday. We _____ gone out.

   (A) are supposed to . . . had to have   (C) may have . . . could not have

   (B) should have . . . could have   (D) must have . . . should have

9. Jason _____ new grass in his front yard because bugs had killed his old lawn.

   (A) had to put down   (C) may have put down

   (B) used to put down   (D) would have put down

10. Kenny _____, but he never even called.

    (A) would have stop by   (C) was supposed to stop by

    (B) must have stopped by   (D) is going to stop by

Part C Read each sentence. Look at the underlined part. If it is correct, circle C. If it is wrong, circle X, and write the correct form on the line. Five of the sentences are wrong.

C (X) 1. When Bobby was a little boy, he <u>didn't could whistle</u>.

_____

C X 2. My brother and I <u>used to take</u> piano lessons on Saturdays.

_____

C X 3. I'm a little worried. I <u>should have left</u> the iron on.

_____

C X 4. You <u>couldn't have called</u> me at 10:00. You were on the boat until 11:00.

_____

C X 5. In the old days, women <u>would wear tight corsets</u> to make their waists look slimmer.

_____

C X 6. I <u>shouldn't have taken</u> so long to answer each question. I ran out of time.

_____

C X 7. Ted <u>had to discontinue</u> his cable service because he couldn't afford the expense.

_____

C X 8. I can't believe you got here so quickly. You <u>may have driven</u> all night.

_____ is _____

C X 9. The parade <u>supposed to start</u> at 2:00, but the weather may postpone it.

_____ to _____

C X 10. Paul <u>is going go</u> to graduate school after he gets his bachelor's degree.

_____

TEST 85 Subject-Verb Agreement

Clear Grammar 4, Unit 9

Name _____ Date _____

Part A Circle the subjects that take singular verbs.

everyone	five hundred students	the United States	the team
dancing	each of the students	a lot of people	traffic
mountains	a number of people	the furniture	the news
politics	all of the money	Alaska and Hawaii	the newspaper

Part B Check for subject-verb agreement. Circle the answer that correctly completes each sentence.

1. The movie about Shrek and his friends (was, were) interesting.

2. Here (is, are) the application forms. Please fill them out completely.

3. The students each (has, have) to do a presentation.

4. Everyone (is bringing, are bringing) his or her favorite recipe.

5. That show about whales (was, were) really fascinating.

6. Learning foreign languages (takes, take) time and practice.

7. James Taylor and Van Morrison (is, are) two of my favorite singers.

8. My family (is, are) very close.

9. Neither of the computer classes (offers, offer) what I am looking for.

10. Most of us in this class (speaks, speak) more than one language.

11. Dancing to salsa and merengue (is, are) great exercise.

12. Linguistics (is, are) the study of language.

13. All of the candidates (has, have) strengths and weaknesses.

14. Rollerblading and bicycling (is, are) my hobbies.

15. Takahiro is the tall guy talking with those men who (is, are) wearing baseball uniforms.

16. One of my friends (is, are) going to spend two years in Nepal with the Peace Corps.

17. Yana is the only one of my friends that (is, are) married already.

18. Some of the people who (works, work) there want to go on strike for better wages.

19. Our mail (arrives, arrive) early every morning.

20. There (is, are) 50 stars on the American flag to represent the 50 states.

TEST 86 Subject-Verb Agreement

Clear Grammar 4, Unit 9

Name _____   Date _____

Part A Fill in the blanks with the correct form of the verb in parentheses. Make sure the subject and verb agree. Follow the example.

Example: Macaroni and cheese (be) ___is___ Tommy's favorite food.

1. A caterpillar (make) _____ a cocoon around itself.

2. Gold (increase) _____ in value over time.

3. Jan and Dean (be going) _____ to Portland on Friday.

4. Miguel (have worked) _____ with computers for 15 years.

5. You and your husband (ought to come) _____ to our house for dinner.

6. My brother (can help) _____ you move your furniture.

7. The deadline to pay the ticket (be) _____ June 30th.

8. (Be) _____ there anything I can do to help you?

9. Most of the people (agree) _____ with the water restrictions.

10. Rock and roll music (have been) _____ popular since the 1950s.

Part B Circle the letter of the answer that correctly completes each sentence.

1. Several _____ a nest outside my front door.

   (A) wasps were building   (C) wasps was building

   (B) wasps are build   (D) wasp are building

2. _____ a subject that Ben can't discuss without getting angry.

   (A) Politics are   (C) Are politics

   (B) Politics is   (D) Is politics

3. _____ dinner together every night.

   (A) Our family eat   (C) Our family eats

   (B) Do our family eat   (D) Does our family eat

4. _____ Ellen or Dave _____ going to bring the textbooks to my house.

   (A) Either . . . are   (C) Either . . . is

   (B) Is . . . either   (D) Are . . . either

Clear Grammar 4

5. _____ the lottery every week.

    (A) Someone win   (C) Does someone win

    (B) Do someone win   (D) Someone wins

6. The women and children each _____ their life preservers.

    (A) have to put on   (C) has to put on

    (B) have to putting on   (D) have putting on

7. _____ an illness that is accompanied by a rash on the skin.

    (A) Measles are   (C) Measles is

    (B) Measles were   (D) Measles was

8. _____ there many opportunities for advancement in your company?

    (A) Is   (C) Are

    (B) Was   (D) Have

9. The Miami Dolphins _____ the football team that won the Super Bowl in 1970.

    (A) is   (C) are

    (B) have   (D) am

10. _____ anybody _____ what time it is?

    (A) Does . . . knows   (C) Do . . . know

    (B) Does . . . know   (D) Do . . . knows

Part C   Underline the form of the verb that correctly completes each sentence.

1. The children (play, plays) outside during recess.

2. Much of the ice (were, was) melted by the time the picnic ended.

3. Dan's furniture (were, was) put in storage until his house was built.

4. Mike (will keep, wills keep) my kitten while I'm on vacation.

5. Saturn is the only one of the planets that (have, has) rings around it.

6. (Do, Does) your parents call you often?

7. Every citizen (have, has) the right to vote.

8. Neither George nor his neighbor (knows, know) why the electricity is out.

9. Both Sonny and Cheryl (has, have) lucrative singing careers.

10. Annie and Chris (should, shoulds) be here soon.

TEST 87   Review of Prepositions

Clear Grammar 4, Unit 10

Name _____   Date _____

Part A Find 17 preposition mistakes, and underline them. Write the correct prepositions above the mistake. Follow the example.

Example: Barbara and Ralph live <u>at</u> Marietta, Georgia.
(in)

My parents are soon going to celebrate their 40th anniversary of wedding. I've looked for their wedding pictures many times since I was a child, and those photos tell the story of that special day. My mom and dad got married at Key West, Florida, on a little church in Simonton Street at 11 A.M. in February 17th. My mom looked beautiful on her white dress as she walked down the aisle toward my dad. On her hands, she was holding a white roses' bouquet. My mom and dad looked for each other with eyes full from love as they said "I do" and put the wedding rings at each other's fingers. After the ceremony, as they walked out from the church as husband and wife, their friends threw rice in them. At the reception, everyone danced and ate and celebrated. Later, my parents left to start their honeymoon, looking forward for their new life together. Now, they have been married with each for almost 40 years and have two grown-up daughters, my sister and I, and we are planning a ruby anniversary party as a surprise to them.

Part B Answer the following questions in complete sentences. Each sentence should contain an appropriate preposition. Circle the preposition that you use. Follow the example.

Example: Where do you live? _____ *I live (in) Seattle, Washington.* _____

1. How do you communicate with your friends and relatives? (letter, phone, e-mail, etc.)

   _____

2. With what utensils do Japanese people usually eat?

   _____

3. What time do you usually get up in the mornings?

   _____

4. Where would you rather live—a big city or a small town? Why?

   _____

5. What is something you're proud of?

   _____

6. Where do you keep important documents at home?

   _____

7. When is your favorite program on TV?

   _____

8. If you could live anywhere in the world, where would you like to live and why?

   _____

Clear Grammar 4, Unit 10

Name _____ Date _____

Part A Read these sentences carefully, and underline the correct words.

1. Our graduation is (in, on, at) 6:00 (in, on, at) the 7th.

2. Jay was (in, up, at) hot water because he didn't call his parents to tell them he would be late.

3. Hank's plane arrived (in, out, at) Germany on June 19th.

4. After several warnings, Shawn's boss finally told him to shape (in, up, on) or ship (out, off, under).

5. Lee and Chuck traveled (with, by, in) car to their children's house in Ohio.

6. Luis made an appointment (for, by, to) speak to his son's principal.

7. Barbara spread the icing on the cake (by, for, with) a plastic spatula.

8. (For, In order to, By) see better, Michelle and Lane sat in the front row of the theater.

9. Most parents don't approve (to, of, about) their children's underage drinking.

10. Some of the streets (in, on, at) San Francisco remind me (for, to, of) Venice, Italy.

11. Does this dictionary belong (in, about, to) you?

12. My classmates and I look forward (in, about, to) the end of the semester.

13. Ginny was angry (at, about, from) her father for forgetting her birthday.

14. Elvis Presley was famous (in, about, for) wearing lavish costumes.

15. Giving (in, up, for) smoking is very challenging for people who have the courage to try it.

Part B Circle the letter of the answer that correctly completes each sentence.

1. Nancy _____ her children as they played in the park.

   (A) kept an eye in   (C) kept an eye at

   (B) kept an eye on   (D) kept an eye for

2. Dennis _____ to help his mother around the house.

   (A) bend over backwards   (C) bends over backwards

   (B) bend up backwards   (D) bends to backwards

3. _____ different world religions?

   (A) You are familiar with   (C) You are familiar to

   (B) Are you familiar on   (D) Are you familiar with

4. Olga _____ her son because he is in the military.

   (A) are worried about   (C) is worried to

   (B) are worried for   (D) is worried about

5. Would you please help me _____ my keys? I can't find them anywhere.

   (A) look for   (C) look at

   (B) look on   (D) look in

6. This dessert _____ three ingredients: chocolate, flour, and eggs.

   (A) consists in   (C) consists at

   (B) consists for   (D) consists of

7. Barry went to an employment agency _____ explore all his options.

   (A) for   (C) in order to

   (B) with   (D) by

8. Irene wrote her entire paper _____ because her computer was broken.

   (A) by hand   (C) with hand

   (B) of hand   (D) at hand

9. _____ school especially early on my first day.

   (A) I arrived in   (C) I arrived on

   (B) I arrived at   (D) I arrived for

10. The Sears Tower is the tallest building _____ Chicago.

    (A) in   (C) at

    (B) on   (D) for

11. Ed and Lisa listened _____ the guitar player and enjoyed the sound _____ the music.

    (A) of . . . to   (C) to . . . in

    (B) to . . . of   (D) at . . . for

12. Pam wanted to _____ her weekend chores, so she woke up early _____ Saturday.

    (A) get a jump of . . . on   (C) get a jump on . . . on

    (B) get a jump out . . . at   (D) get a jump off . . . in

13. Linda is _____ math, but she is very good at writing.

   (A) bad to   (C) bad on

   (B) bad for   (D) bad at

14. Beth has been _____ Irving _____ 30 years.

   (A) married with . . . in   (C) married by . . . with

   (B) married to . . . for   (D) married in . . . to

15. Seymour is _____ all of his children's accomplishments.

   (A) proud of   (C) proud by

   (B) proud for   (D) proud with

TEST 89 Review of Verb Tenses

Clear Grammar Book 4, Unit 11

Name _____   Date _____

Read each statement carefully, and then underline the correct verb tense.

1. The apprehensive players on the determined team and the coach (are, were) greatly relieved when the buzzer sounded and the game was finally over.

2. In contrast to what was previously thought, historians now agree that Abraham Lincoln (has, had) a great deal of experience as a lawyer.

3. Included in any good list of current favorite tourist destinations to Europe (are, were, had been) Paris, Berlin, and Madrid.

4. Contrary to previous studies, a recent university study (has concluded, had concluded) that it is not dangerous for pregnant women to drink as many as two cups of coffee a day.

5. The labor unions (will meet, met, have been meeting) with management all last night in order to avoid a paralyzing strike.

6. Long regarded as one of the leading figures in the development of the short story, O. Henry (is, will be) the author of many well-known American favorites, including "The Gift of the Magi" and "The Last Leaf."

7. *Just Another City Person,* Robert Luden's newest novel, is an inspiring story about a young immigrant who (had tried, tried) to create a new life for himself and his family in New York City.

8. According to the most recent reports, investigators now believe that the tragic accident (has been, was) caused by pilot error.

9. The information on the post office website explains that postage for mailing a parcel (varies, varied) according to its weight, size, and destination.

10. Abundant water power (is, was, has been) quite an important factor in the rapid transformation of New Hampshire into an industrial state very early in its history.

Clear Grammar 4

TEST 90 Review of Verb Tenses

Clear Grammar Book 4, Unit 11

Name _____   Date _____

Read each statement carefully, and then underline the correct verb tense.

1. How aspirin really (was working, works, worked) inside our bodies and our brains is a mystery to doctors even today.

2. To avoid food poisoning, uncooked food (must be, must have been) kept refrigerated.

3. The method of house construction in a given area depends mainly on what kinds of materials (are, were, had been) readily available.

4. Although accurate records are not available, it is thought that approximately 6,000 (drown, drowned, were drowning) in the hurricane that hit Galveston, Texas, in 1900.

5. At the present time, some scientists (are believing, believed, believe) that the heating of the earth's atmosphere may be caused by volcanoes or some other natural reason.

6. Founded in 1701, Philadelphia (is, will be, is being) not only the largest city in the state of Pennsylvania but also one of the largest cities in the entire United States.

7. The great magician Houdini (attempts, was attempting, had attempted, attempted) several times to find out whether there is life after death, but even he himself died without finding the answer.

8. There are several countries in the world such as Madagascar and Cuba that (consist, are consisting, consisted) of only one island with a handful of smaller ones.

9. Because students lead such busy lives these days, some educators (insist, had insisted, insisted, were insisting) on giving as little homework as possible to their students while others assign the maximum amount.

10. Feudalism, a system of military and political organization based on land ownership, (has lasted, had lasted, had been lasting, lasted) until the end of the 13th century.

Clear Grammar 4, Units 2–11

Name _____   Date _____

Part A Word forms. Use the indicated form of the word in a sentence. Follow the example.

Example: capitalize (noun) ___*We studied the rules for capitalization.*___

1. color (adjective) _____

2. danger (adjective) _____

3. work (noun) _____

4. complete (adverb) _____

5. happy (noun) _____

6. dark (verb)_____

7. understand (adjective) _____

8. perform (noun) _____

9. art (noun) _____

10. final (verb)_____

Part B Past perfect. Combine the statements into one sentence using the given time phrases. Change any verbs necessary. Follow the example.

Example: We decided to get married. We knew each other for two years. (before)

___*Before we decided to get married, we had known each other for two years.*___

1. Alberto was 30. He lived in 15 different countries. (by the time)

   _____

2. Summer officially started. The temperature was already in the 90s every day. (a month before)

   _____

3. Scott got to the party at midnight. Almost everyone went home. (when)

   _____

Clear Grammar 4

4. We arrived at the beach ready to swim. Someone spotted a shark. (Just before)

_____

5. Nelson Mandela was a civil rights activist and a political prisoner. He became President of South Africa. (before)

_____

Part C Conditionals (*if / wish*), adverb clauses, noun clauses, reduction of clauses, past modals, subject-verb agreement, review of prepositions. Underline the correct answer. Follow the example.

> *Example:* The car (park, <u>parked</u>, parking) behind yours in the driveway is mine.
>
> I parked there (if, when, <u>because</u>) I didn't want to park on the street.

1. Children shouldn't be allowed to watch movies or TV programs (contain, containing, contained) excessive violence.

2. I wish you (will tell, told, had told) me. I (would have, should have, must have) helped you.

3. Could you tell me where (is the principal's office, the principal's office is)?

4. Along the road (leads, leading) to New Smyrna Beach, there (is, are) beautiful pink and white oleander bushes.

5. One of the neurolinguistics researchers I met at the conference (lives, live) right here in Orlando.

6. Vic says (what, that, than) if he (wins, won) the lottery, he (would, should) quit his job, buy a house on the beach, and fish all day.

7. Your homework (was, were) late again, and you missed another test. Do you realize (how, what, that) effect this will have on your final grade?

8. Look at you; you're soaking wet! You (should have, must have, might have) forgotten your umbrella today. Go upstairs, take (out, off, over) those wet clothes, and take a hot shower.

9. We are counting (in, on, of) you to take care (of, for, about) the greenhouses (during, since, while) we're in Denver.

10. If I (am, was, were) you, I (will, would, am going to) buy a car (rate, rating, rated) highly by *Consumer Reports* magazine.

11. Each of you (is, are) going to practice buddy breathing and mask removal-replacement, two important safety procedures. (Is, Are) there any questions before we begin?

12. Some of the students in the algebra class (was, were) confused (on, with, about) the assignment, but if they (paid, had paid) attention while the teacher was explaining it, they (wouldn't of, wouldn't have) had any problem.

13. (If, Whether, Because) we want to or not, most of us (has, have) to work for a living.

14. Those students (qualify, qualifying) for scholarships will be notified by the end of the month.

15. (When, While, Before) you (was, were) young, did you (use to, used to) catch fireflies on summer evenings?

Clear Grammar 4, Units 2–11

Name _____   Date _____

Part A Read these sentences carefully, and underline the correct words.

1. By the time Tom got to the airport, the plane (had arrived, arrived, is arriving).

2. I (hadn't had, hadn't have, didn't had) the chance to ask any questions before the meeting ended.

3. Bob Dylan is a talented (musician, musicean, musicer).

4. Juliet has (curly, curlful, curlate) hair.

5. If you don't call me tonight, I (assumed, will assume, have assumed) that you won't be coming over.

6. If Josie (had, has, have) time, she would take yoga classes.

7. If you (had, will, may have) asked for a ride to school, I (could have, might, can have) given you one.

8. (Before, So that, As long as) the concert started, the crowd waited in line to get inside.

9. Kevin believes (that, who, what) the judgment will be passed in his favor.

10. Mary plans to retire when she's 65 (even if, only if, however) she doesn't have a lot of money saved up.

11. Statistics show (that, what, who) people are living longer than they did 50 years ago.

12. Did you understand (who, what, that) the teacher said?

13. I'm not sure if I can lend you any money. I (may have, must have, should have) spent it all at the grocery store.

14. Last night my father (wasn't able to, can't, couldn't have) fall asleep.

15. (Despite the fact that, Given that, Although) he was able to get a job, Jeremy should be able to start saving money.

16. The lion, the scarecrow, and the tin man (is, am, are) three characters in *The Wizard of Oz*.

17. Hot dogs and hamburgers (is, are, am) popular cookout foods.

18. When he was satisfied (for, with, in) his report, Randy gave it to his boss.

19. Non-smokers are opposed (for, to, by) having to share space with smokers.

20. The judge declared the defendant to be guilty (of, for, with) robbery.

Part B Read each sentence carefully. Look at the underlined part. If the underlined part is correct, circle C. If the underlined part is wrong, circle X, and write the correct answer on the line. Eight of the sentences are wrong.

C   X   1.   The United Nations has scheduled a meeting for next month.

_____

C   X   2.   The islands of Puerto Rico and Haiti are in the Caribbean._____

C   X   3.   Mandy has slept for 11 hours before her alarm clock rang. _____

C   X   4.   Lorna no had finished cooking dinner when her guests arrived. _____

C   X   5.   During their discussive, Brad and Ed made valid points._____

C   X   6.   Dogs have a reputation for being faithful animals._____

C   X   7.   If I don't get this job, I will to be upset._____

C   X   8.   If I was you, I would take my car to the shop._____

C   X   9.   You ought have sent a thank-you note to the hostess. _____

C   X   10.   Since the park was closed, we went to the mall._____

C   X   11.   The milk was sour despite of the fact that I had just bought it.

_____

C   X   12.   Jason loves his children whether or not he agrees with them.

_____

C   X   13.   Bob was so sleepy that he could barely keep his eyes open. _____

C   X   14.   Can you tell me where is the jewelry department? _____

C   X   15.   The Golden Gate Bridge, located in California, is a popular tourist site.

_____

Part C Circle the letter of the answer that correctly completes each sentence.

1. The faucet _____ all night when my husband finally turned it off.

   (A) were dripping

   (B) had been dripping

   (C) has been dripping

   (D) has dripped

2. Kelly _____ well until her son came home from overseas.

   (A) hadn't been sleeping

   (B) hasn't been slept

   (C) had slept

   (D) has slept

3. Brian spoke _____ to his young son and tried to calm his nerves.

   (A) quiet

   (B) quietish

   (C) quietly

   (D) quietful

4. The key to a successful _____ is good _____.

   (A) relationship . . . communicate

   (B) relation . . . communicate

   (C) relation . . . communicative

   (D) relationship . . . communication

5. Jack _____ more money if he _____ to stay home more often.

   (A) could has saved . . . chose

   (B) could have saved . . . had chosen

   (C) could have saved . . . chooses

   (D) could save . . . chosen

6. I wish _____ to stop working for a little while.

   (A) I was able

   (B) I can

   (C) I were able

   (D) I can be able

7. Troy will graduate in the spring _____ the classes he needs are offered.

   (A) provided that

   (B) although

   (C) even though

   (D) even if

8. William didn't see _____ before the accident happened.

   (A) where were the other cars

   (B) when the other cars

   (C) where the other cars were

   (D) how were the other cars

9. It is remarkable that nobody was hurt _____ they weren't wearing seatbelts.

   (A) only if

   (B) given that

   (C) unless

   (D) so that

10. In his notes, President Kennedy wrote that _____ about the missile crisis.

    (A) was he worried   (C) he was worried

    (B) he is worried   (D) is he worried

11. Larry asked his parents _____ him sleep at his friend's house.

    (A) so they would let   (C) would they let

    (B) whether they would let   (D) unless they would let

12. My feet _____ from all the hiking we did.

    (A) was aching   (C) am aching

    (B) is aching   (D) were aching

13. A number of people _____ outside the voting area waiting to cast their votes.

    (A) am standing   (C) was standing

    (B) were standing   (D) is standing

14. The manager insists that all timecards _____ at the end of the week.

    (A) be turned in   (C) are turning in

    (B) are turn in   (D) turned in

15. When he was a little boy, Armando _____ English without an accent.

    (A) couldn't speak   (C) can't speak

    (B) isn't able to speak   (D) won't speak

TEST 93   General Review of Advanced English Grammar

Name _____   Date _____

Circle the one underlined part that has a grammatical error. Write your correction above the error.

1. Chemicals <u>dumping</u> in the river are polluting the water <u>so quickly that</u> the water <u>may not</u> be able to support <u>any life</u> within a year.

2. The <u>South American country</u> of Uruguay <u>is about</u> the same size <u>than</u> the state of Washington <u>in the</u> United States.

3. The police <u>feel that</u> the newspaper reports have consistently <u>exaggerate</u> the <u>actual number</u> of <u>crimes</u> in the area.

4. The <u>cloths</u> that the local people in <u>tropical</u> countries <u>wear are</u> usually lightweight <u>and cool</u> due to the climate.

5. Because St. Petersburg, also <u>known as</u> Leningrad when it was part of the former Soviet Union, has one of the best <u>art museum</u> in the world, it is <u>experiencing</u> a surge in interest by <u>international art lovers</u>.

6. For someone who wants to write <u>children's books</u>, a great deal of imagination <u>requires</u> as <u>well as</u> an understanding of how children <u>see</u> the world.

7. While snow often falls <u>in north</u> part of the state, <u>such</u> weather <u>rarely</u> if ever <u>occurs</u> in the rest of the state.

8. Though Elvis Presley <u>has</u> died several years ago <u>in</u> Tennessee, some of his <u>most devoted</u> fans still cling to the belief <u>that he is alive</u>.

9. <u>While</u> the police <u>still do not know</u> exactly what <u>was</u> happened, it is <u>reported that</u> two suspects in the case have been taken into custody.

10. <u>Sneezing</u> is one <u>of</u> the <u>body's</u> natural <u>response</u> to the environment.

TEST 94 General Review of Advanced English Grammar

Name _____   Date _____

Circle the one underlined part that has a grammatical error. Write your correction above the error.

1. The writing style and the dialogues in *Charity of the Gods*, the new book by Otis Redmann, are unlike his another books.

2. Rising from an earliest job as a newspaper boy, he eventually became the chief editor of the entire newspaper.

3. According to a report in a recent edition of a travel magazine, many people who fly frequently prefer the Boeing 747 jumbo jet because of it's comfort and safety record.

4. Although a baseball is about the same size than a tennis ball, the former is heavier and harder than the latter is.

5. Students in a beginning language course often have a great deal of homework, but many of this is actually listening work to be done in the laboratory.

6. As well as being an important port, New Orleans is also a popular tourist destinations.

7. The instructor informed Jason and I that our papers were not up to her standards and that we would have to write them again.

8. Many theories abound, but still no one has been able to explain the mysteries which taken place in the area of the Atlantic Ocean known as the Bermuda Triangle.

9. As soon as you will reach home tomorrow, please call to let me know that you have arrived there safely.

10. The hotel guests complained for the lack of clean towels, the bugs in the rooms, and the hot water that trickled out of the faucets; however, none was angry enough to leave the hotel.

101 Clear Grammar Tests **TEST 94**   213

Advanced Grammar

TEST 95 General Review of Advanced English Grammar

Name _____   Date _____

Circle the one underlined part that has a grammatical error. Write your correction above the error.

1. It is a <u>common</u> misconception <u>that</u> twins <u>always look</u> <u>like</u>.

2. Although <u>the</u> television could be of great <u>educational</u> value, many sociologists <u>fear</u> that it <u>became</u> a replacement for human contact.

3. The <u>increase</u> use of computers <u>has had</u> a major <u>impact on</u> education by <u>changing</u> the traditional role of both the teacher and the textbook.

4. By the time Halley's comet comes racing <u>across</u> the <u>night</u> sky again, most of <u>the</u> people alive today will <u>pass</u> away.

5. With little or <u>none</u> food available, <u>many</u> of <u>the</u> people in that area <u>may</u> starve.

6. Even before work <u>was to begin</u> on the new airport in Hong Kong, <u>the Chinese government</u> in Beijing complained <u>about</u> the <u>estimating</u> cost.

7. <u>The</u> sculptor Chares <u>completed</u> the Colossus of Rhodes, <u>a statue bronze</u> of the Roman god Apollo, <u>in</u> 280 B.C.

8. According to the passport office, <u>there</u> is necessary to submit two small photographs as well as a <u>completed</u> application form to its office <u>at least three weeks</u> before the <u>approximate departure date</u>.

9. On the stove were an <u>aluminum small</u> pot, a <u>dirty frying pan</u>, and an old spatula, but there <u>were no</u> dishes anywhere <u>in the</u> kitchen.

10. Alexander Bell's telephone <u>was first</u> device <u>that allowed</u> the transmission of <u>the</u> human voice to a distant place in a two-way conversation <u>format</u>.

Name _____   Date _____

Circle the one underlined part that has a grammatical error. Write your correction above the error.

1. Columbus, long <u>regarded as</u> a hero but recently <u>criticized by</u> historians and sociologists, was <u>born in</u> 1451 and <u>was</u> died in 1506.

2. Though she studied <u>all the</u> night, she <u>did not pass</u> the test because she had neither attended class consistently <u>nor</u> applied <u>herself</u> during the semester.

3. The fire destroyed <u>most of the</u> building, but <u>fortunately</u> very <u>few</u> of the large equipment was <u>damaged</u>.

4. <u>Like</u> most other Southeast Asian countries, Thailand has benefited from trade with other countries <u>because of its location and resources</u>; unlike its <u>neighbor's</u>, however, it <u>was</u> never colonized.

5. <u>Never has the world's climate</u> been so chaotic <u>and</u> unpredictable <u>that</u> it is <u>at</u> present.

6. The supervising teacher <u>in</u> any department in a school is responsible <u>for</u> the <u>teaching</u> materials that the teachers <u>needed</u> for their classes.

7. <u>Each</u> of the singers in the <u>music</u> contest receives <u>total score</u> based <u>on</u> several factors, including voice control and pitch range.

8. <u>In order to import</u> certain <u>good</u> into a country, it is necessary to file various forms and <u>pay</u> a certain <u>duty, a kind of tax</u>.

9. <u>Afterward Laos</u> became a French protectorate <u>in</u> 1893, <u>it was</u> included <u>in the</u> union of Indochina.

10. Harry Truman <u>returned his</u> home <u>in</u> Missouri <u>to write</u> his memoirs after <u>leaving the</u> White House.

Name _____   Date _____

Circle the one underlined part that has a grammatical error. Write your correction above the error.

1. It has <u>been</u> suggested that <u>much of</u> Edgar Allen <u>Poe's writing</u> was <u>did</u> while he was under the influence of alcohol or drugs.

2. Due to <u>the increase</u> in security <u>problems</u>, airplane passengers <u>must to show</u> their passports <u>when boarding</u> international flights.

3. Recent <u>evidence suggestion</u> that meat and other foods must <u>be cooked</u> at a temperature <u>of at least 155 degrees</u> Fahrenheit <u>in order to kill</u> the *E. coli* bacteria.

4. Current statistics indicate that the population of the Philippines <u>is</u> increasing <u>so</u> rapidly <u>than that</u> of Japan <u>or Canada</u>.

5. <u>Alike</u> fish, dolphins have fins <u>to steer</u> themselves in the water and <u>use</u> swimming for their primary mode of movement; <u>however</u>, dolphins are not fish.

6. After the <u>three-hour examination</u>, the students were <u>mental</u> exhausted and <u>wanted to do nothing</u> but <u>relax</u> for a few hours.

7. <u>By the time</u> Orville Wright died <u>in</u> 1948, there <u>will have</u> been <u>much</u> progress in aviation.

8. When Gerald Ford became <u>the</u> 38th U.S. President in 1974, it <u>did</u> the first time <u>that</u> a person became President without <u>being elected</u>.

9. <u>Comparing</u> to the mayor's plan, the city council's plan offers <u>many</u> more advantages <u>for</u> the people <u>living</u> in that area of the city.

10. In 1862, <u>in order</u> to support <u>the</u> Civil War, Congress <u>begun</u> the <u>nation's</u> first income tax.

decrease over the summer. 3. Bradley caught a cold, so he has to take medicine. 4. How far is it from New York to California? 5. C 6. Jay's mother allowed him to spend the night at a friend's house. 7. C 8. The lasagna was so delicious that I decided to have another piece. 9. C 10. C 11. Tina was lucky that her car didn't stall on a deserted road. 12. C 13. It's a beautiful day today. The sun is shining, and the air is cool. 14. I tore my shirt on this nail, so I have to change it before we go out. 15. C 16. C 17. Before the baseball game, the people sang their [or the] national anthem. 18. There were two President Roosevelts in U.S. history. One was Franklin, and the other was Theodore. 19. C 20. C PART B. 1. The 2. likes 3. didn't understand 4. How often do 5. is always 6. me 7. yours 8. Others 9. the smartest 10. must not 11. Most 12. The 13. is going to 14. wore 15. How deep 16. is usually 17. them 18. Who's 19. the saddest 20. may PART C. 1. C 2. B 3. C 4. B 5. C 6. A 7. C 8. B 9. D 10. C

Test 49 PART A. 1. f 2. d 3. j 4. g 5. c 6. e 7. b 8. a 9. i 10. h PART B. 1. C 2. C 3. A 4. A 5. D PART C. 1. out 2. up 3. after 4. on 5. out PART D. 1. X, try them on 2. C 3. X, figure it out 4. C 5. C

Test 50 PART A. 1. up 2. out 3. up 4. out 5. up [or on] 6. back 7. up 8. up . . . out 9. away 10. on PART B. 1. C 2. A 3. D 4. B 5. A 6. D 7. C 8. A 9. D 10. C. PART C. 1. broke down . . . get off 2. called her back 3. Look out for 4. gave up 5. give it back 6. ran out of 7. hold on 8. turned on 9. put up with 10. hand in

Test 51 PART A. 1. was taking, called 2. did 3. met, was living 4. liked 5. Were you 6. was planning, lost 7. was waiting, saw 8. left 9. Did you enjoy 10. was baking, was washing [or washed] PART B. 1. attended, was attending 2. was sleeping, slept 3. was throwing, threw 4. played, were playing 5. sent, sent

Test 52 PART A. 1. was listening; heard; didn't know; asked; explained; showed 2. went; bought; traveled; decided; were hiking; continued; returned; had; were flying PART B. 1. was reading 2. read 3. were reading 4. was sleeping 5. slept 6. Were . . . sleeping 7. worked 8. was working 9. did work 10. dropped PART C. Answers will vary but should use appropriate tense. 1. Answer should be past progressive. 2. Answer should be simple past. 3. Answer should be past progressive. 4. Answer should be simple past. 5. Answer should be past progressive.

Test 53 PART A. 1. been 2. worked 3. studied 4. thought 5. told 6. written 7. bought 8. gone 9. spoken 10. drunk 11. done 12. heard 13. given 14. talked 15. broken 16. cooked 17. flown 18. read 19. taken 20. had PART B. 1. have . . . finished 2. went / Have . . . gone / have been 3. Have . . . cooked / made 4. Have . . . gotten / have heard 5. Has . . . tried / tried 6. have seen / have seen 7. Has . . . left / left 8. Has . . . finished / haven't finished 9. have . . . been / have been / got 10. have . . . eaten / have eaten / ate

Test 54 PART A. 1. Have . . . won 2. did . . . begin 3. Have . . . thought . . . haven't . . . had 4. did . . . cost 5. have told . . . forgot 6. drank 7. spent . . . decided 8. has lost 9. have done 10. felt PART B. 1. X, went to 2. X, has run 3. C 4. C 5. X, have been 6. X, hasn't left 7. C 8. C 9. X, I have never forgotten 10. C PART C. 1. C 2. B 3. B 4. D 5. C 6. A 7. C 8. D 9. C 10. D

Test 55 PART A. 1. slowly 2. well 3. fast 4. lovely . . . quiet 5. bad . . . clearly 6. by train 7. by forming 8. poor . . . by not paying 9. with 10. creative PART B. the, lately, easy, correct, quick. hardly, well.

Test 56 PART A. 1. hard . . . suddenly 2. quickly 3. nervous 4. careful 5. quietly 6. patient . . . clearly 7. easily . . . good 8. fluent 9. well 10. important . . . promptly 11. loud 12. excitedly 13. strong 14. carelessly 15. politely . . . angry PART B. 1. to 2. by 3. With 4. with 5. By 6. to 7. with 8. by 9. by 10 with

Test 57 PART A. 1. for 2. to 3. of 4. about 5. of 6. for 7. at 8. with 9. for 10. to PART B. to, used to, to, to, for, in, to, about

Test 58 PART A. 1. for . . . on 2. to . . . with 3. of . . . in 4. for . . . from 5. about 6. of 7. of . . . to 8. of . . . to 9. of 10 to . . . about PART B. Answers will vary but should utilize the correct preposition. 1. at --- 2. for --- 3. with --- 4. in --- 5. to --- 6. of --- 7. about --- 8. for --- 9. about/with --- 10. with ---

Test 59 PART A. 1. will be 2. were recalled 3. must be kept 4. has been changed 5. was donated 6. is requested 7. have been posted 8. should be finished PART B. 1. was born 2. built 3. is scheduled 4. exciting 5. tired of 6. shocked 7. will be announced 8. fascinating 9. died 10. surprising, was posted 11. was 12. agreed, handpainted

Test 60 PART A. 1. would be called 2. was being towed 3. are cleaned 4. is going to be built 5. is prepared 6. was written 7. should be provided 8. was used 9. was . . . being cooked 10. has been celebrated PART B. 1. X 2. X 3. C 4. C 5. X 6. X 7. C 8. X 9. C 10. C PART C. 1. with 2. to 3. by/with 4. about 5. in/with

Test 61 PART A.
On Friday nights my family likes to go to a restaurant (that, <u>which</u>, who) is near our home. The woman (that, which, <u>who</u>) owns the restaurant is from a town in Thailand (that, <u>which</u>, who) is near the Laotian and Cambodian borders. The meals (that, <u>which</u>, who) she serves represent the traditional foods of her homeland, as well as the foods (that, <u>which</u>, who) were brought to her town by people from neighboring countries (that, <u>which</u>, who) had to leave their homes during the Vietnam War. She learned to cook many types of food and brought all of the recipes with her when she came to the U.S. My family feels sorry for the people (who's, <u>whose</u>) lives were affected by the war, and we are honored to have the opportunity to eat delicious international meals (that, <u>which</u>, who) are available so close to our home. PART B. 1. My son

who [*or* that] lives in Boston is coming home for Thanksgiving. 2. Kayla bought the leather jacket that [*or* which] was on sale. 3. Have you seen the new reality show that [*or* which] was filmed in Puerto Rico? 4. Everyone enjoyed the pumpkin pie that [*or* which] Marina baked. 5. You should go to the dance club that [*or* which] used to be a train station on River Street. 6. The security guard who [*or* that] knows my brother helped me when I locked my keys in my car. 7. Did your parents send you the money that [*or* which] you needed the money to pay your tuition?

Test 62 PART A. 1. that, which, ø 2. who, whom, that, ø 3. that, which 4. that, which 5. whose 6. that, which 7. that, which, ø 8. that, which, ø 9. who 10. that, which 11. that, which 12. that, which 13. who, that 14. that, which 15. that, which PART B. 1. My cousin is a dentist who/that works with young children. 2. People who/that graduate from college will make more money over their lifetime than non-college graduates. 3. The employees who/that got raises are very happy. 4. I always mix up the two words *por* and *para*, that/which mean *for* in Spanish. 5. My cousin lives in Cartagena, Colombia, which is a beautiful old city that is/ø surrounded by castle walls and looks like a bigger version of St. Augustine, Florida.

Test 63 PART A. 1. sleeping 2. bowling 3. to sell 4. working 5. to graduate 6. driving 7. to buy 8. to get PART B. 1. would like me to work 2. to stop smoking 3. told him to put 4. want you to show 5. invited me to go 6. look forward to meeting 7. wants us to finish 8. want me to help

Test 64 PART A. 1. to love 2. eating 3. to come 4. to stop . . . smoking . . . doing 5. to go . . . to go 6. both: to drink and drive/drinking and driving, to get 7. having 8. to watch 9. shopping 10. to postpone, wondering 11. camping 12. both: to learn and learning, 13. wearing 14. having 15. cleaning PART B. 1. a gerund; example: Learning to speak a foreign language takes time and patience. 2. infinitive. 3. Answers may vary and may include the following: ask, tell, expect, would like, advise, order, need, permit, teach, allow, force, get, invite, persuade, urge 4. Answers will vary.

Test 65 PART A. Affirmative 1–4. Answers will vary but should correctly use "and . . . too" or "and so . . ." Negative 1–4. Answers will vary but should correctly use "and . . . either" or "and neither . . ." Contrast 1–4. Answers will vary but should correctly use "but . . ." PART B. 1. to [*or* in order to] 2. in order to [*or* to] 3. so 4. However 5. for 6. In order to [*or* to] 7. Therefore 8. to [*or* in order to] 9. for . . . so 10. to

Test 66 PART A. 1. to 2. for 3. did 4. neither 5. however 6. so 7. Therefore 8. so 9. neither 10. in order to PART B. 1. and neither does Tyler, and Tyler doesn't either 2. and so is ice cream, and ice cream is too 3. and so does Ann, and Ann does too 4. and his wife doesn't either, and neither does his wife 5. and so is her family, and her family is too 6. and neither is her daughter, and her daugh-

ter isn't either 7. and so does his Grandpa Joe, and his Grandpa Joe does too 8. and so did her husband, and her husband did too 9. and neither are his friends, and his friends aren't either 10. and Andrea does too, and so does Andrea. PART C. 1. C 2. A 3. B 4. C 5. A 6. C 7. B 8. B 9. C 10. B

Test 67 PART A. 1. to me 2. to me 3. for me 4. to me 5. for me 6. to me 7. for me 8. to me 9. for me 10. to me 11. for me 12. to me PART B. 1. C 2. C 3. X, describe your new car to me 4. C 5. C 6. X, this shirt cost me 7. C 8. X, tell me the answers

Test 68 PART A. 1. a, b 2. b 3. b 4. a 5. b 6. b 7. a, c 8. a, c 9. a 10. c 11. a, c 12. c 13. b 14. a, b 15. a, b 16. b PART B. 1. show 2. explained 3. give 4. sent 5. pass 6. pass 7. says 8. announced

Test 69 PART A. 1. out 2. get information about it 3. depend on them 4. off . . . off 5. up 6. on . . . off 7. up . . . after . . . out for 8. please wait 9. up 10. to distribute or give something to everyone PART B. 1. Have you ever gone 2. had 3. great 4. spent 5. by 6. about 7. so 8. to take 9. were flying 10. intently 11. with 12. took 13. which 14. was made 15. which 16. are estimated 17. to visit 18. in order to 19. haven't been 20. going

Test 70 PART A. 1. X, Turn on 2. C 3. C 4. C 5. X, be responsible for 6. X, is celebrated 7. C 8. C 9. X, bored 10. C 11. X, wants to visit 12. C 13. C 14. C 15. X, talking 16. C 17. X, I like 18. C 19. C 20. X, happy to PART B. 1. B 2. A 3. D 4. C 5. D 6. D 7. C 8. B 9. A 10. C 11. C 12. D 13. D 14. B 15. A PART C. 1. ran out of 2. didn't know 3. has sung 4. hard 5. for 6. died 7. that Tom has 8. to call 9. does 10. for 11. put out 12. When 13. has gone 14. fast 15. happened

Test 71 PART A. 1. b 2. c 3. a 4. c 5. a PART B. 1. Manuel had studied English for six years before he started college in the U.S. 2. Lynn hadn't been working at the company long when she was offered a promotion. 3. Shawn had never experienced an earthquake until she lived in Japan. 4. Before William moved to Texas, he had always lived in the Northwest. 5. They got engaged after they had been dating for just one month. 6. I had been waiting for 35 minutes when the receptionist told me that the doctor wouldn't be able to see me as scheduled. 7. Elizabeth had been married and divorced twice before she turned 24. 8. We didn't join Bob and Sara at the restaurant because we had already eaten dinner at home. 9. The documents had been hidden inside the wall for 100 years before they were found in 1999. 10. Thomas and his friends finally reached New Orleans after they had been driving for 20 hours.

Test 72 PART A. 2. won 3. won 4. became 5. had . . . lived 6. came 7. was 8. came 9. had lived 10. had . . . been 11. gave 12. gave 13. was PART B. 1. When Dan got to the office, he knew that the boss had been looking for him for a while. 2. Gina was thrilled to see her boyfriend because she hadn't seen him for two weeks. 3. Alex had found two seashells before his mother told him to put them down. 4. Elaine and Diane had been shopping for six hours before they found the perfect prom dresses. 5. Marsha went to the doctor because she had not eaten anything for two days. 6. Monica had been to Europe two times before she went there for her wedding. 7. The young couple didn't realize that they had been dancing for hours. 8. Noreen didn't want to go to sleep because she hadn't finished the quilt she was working on. 9. Georgette had been working in customer service for 11 years when she was finally promoted to manager. 10. The pot of water boiled over because I had not been watching it. PART C. 1. C 2. X, had you considered 3. C 4. X, How long had the party been going on 5. C 6. X, hadn't been 7. C 8. X, hadn't prepared 9. X, had been teaching 10. X, Had you known

Test 73 Examples will vary. PART A. *Verbs:* -ize, -ify, -en *Adjectives:* -ish, -less, -ful, -able/-ible, -ous *Nouns:* -ist, -ship, -tion, -ness, -er, -ment, -an/-ian/-ean PART B. 1. rudely . . . rude 2. beautifully . . . beautiful 3. artist . . . artistic 4. pronounce . . . pronunciation 5. impressive . . . impression 6. happiness . . . happily 7. accuracy . . . accurately 8. faithful . . . faithfully 9. dangerous . . . danger 10. help . . . helpful 11. American . . . Americanized 12. stabilize . . . stable 13. interest . . . interesting 14. friend . . . friendship 15. successful . . . succeed

Test 74 PART A. 1. hydrate 2. lessen 3. minimized 4. solidified 5. nervous 6. dependable 7. sugarless 8. medical 9. elusive 10. consultant PART B. 1. C 2. A 3. A 4. C 5. C 6. D 7. C 8. A 9. B 10. A PART C. 1. X, failure 2. C 3. C 4. X, hardship 5. C 6. X, frivolity 7. X, suddenly 8. C 9. X, heroic 10. X, considerate

Test 75 PART A. 1. X, won 2. C 3. C 4. C 5. X, would have studied 6. X, work 7. C 8. C 9. X, prefer 10. C 11. C 12. X, could understand 13. C 14. X, find 15. X, were PART B. Answers will vary but should be logical and use *if* clause and correct verbs. 1. If I won a million dollars, I would . . . 2. If I don't understand [*or* didn't understand] something, I [*or* I would] . . . 3. If I have [*or* had] a headache, I [*or* I would] . . . 4. If I see [*or* saw] a cockroach in my house, I [*or* I would] . . . 5. If I met Brad Pitt, I would . . . PART C. Answers will vary but should use correct structure for sentences with *wish. Examples:* I wish I were/had/could . . .

Test 76 PART A. 1. knew . . . would be 2. needed . . . could [*or* would] light 3. wanted . . . would study 4. spoke . . . would [*or* could] try 5. asked . . . would [*or* could] lend 6. could [*or* would] run . . . trained 7. completed . . . would [*or* could] be 8. saw . . . would not disagree 9. were . . . would try 10. known . . . would have given PART B. 1. will close 2. go 3. would buy 4. would have been 5. would have done 6. were 7. had 8. go 9. will have 10. would have helped PART C. 1. A 2. C 3. B 4. D 5. B 6. A 7. C 8. B 9. C 10. D

Test 77 PART A. 1. He is such a popular singer that people wait in line all day to buy a concert ticket. 2. Please call me as soon as you get this

message./As soon as you get this message, please call me. 3. All workers must pay federal income tax whether they want to or not./Whether they want to or not, all workers must pay federal income tax. 4. You can find friends wherever you go in the world./Wherever you go in the world, you can find friends. 5. Since Sam was a young boy, he has always loved taking care of animals. 6. Georgina has a severe allergic reaction whenever she eats food containing peanuts./Whenever she eats food containing peanuts, Georgina has a severe allergic reaction. 7. I would buy a house in the Greek Islands if I won the lottery./If I won the lottery, I would buy a house in the Greek Islands. 8. My sister is going to take care of our house while we are on vacation in Hawaii./While we are on vacation in Hawaii, my sister is going to take care of our house. 9. Before Ling comes to school in the morning, she studies for one hour. 10. We still receive calls from telemarketers though we registered on the do-not-call list./Though we registered on the do-not-call list, we still receive calls from telemarketers. 11. I like to spend quiet evenings at home, whereas my husband prefers to go out./Whereas my husband prefers to go out, I like to spend quiet evenings at home. 12. Many people want to be bilingual so that they will have better job opportunities. PART B. 1. as 2. If 3. so 4. until 5. where 6. such 7. so that 8. After 9. everywhere 10. Even though 11. While 12. because

Test 78 PART A. 1. After 2. When 3. because 4. Since 5. Although 6. While 7. unless 8. where 9. as if 10. As soon as PART B. 1. C 2. A 3. C 4. B 5. B 6. D 7. D 8. D 9. C 10. B PART C. 1. X, comes 2. C 3. X, by the time 4. X, can 5. C 6. X, we didn't have enough 7. C 8. X, Despite the fact that 9. C 10. C

Test 79 PART A. 1. B 2. A 3. B 4. D 5. B 6. D 7. C PART B. 1. d 2. a 3. h 4. b 5. f 6. c 7. g 8. e

Test 80 PART A. 1. when 2. whether 3. that 4. where 5. where we can 6. how I can 7. where the bank is 8. that 9. How 10. That 11. use 12. study 13. be 14. told 15. had eaten PART B. 1. Women understand that men are complicated people. 2. Our father promised us that we can go to the park on Sunday. 3. Our class learned that Lake Okeechobee is the largest lake in Florida. 4. The weather map indicates that it is going to rain this weekend. 5. We guessed that she was late because she had car trouble. 6. The teacher explained that knowledge of mathematics will benefit us. 7. Scientists have demonstrated that a cure for cancer is possible. 8. The defendant denies that he was in the area at the time of the crime. 9. Studies show that teen drug use is decreasing. 10. The homeowner claims that he was not home when the fire started. PART C. 1. A 2. D 3. D 4. C 5. B 6. C 7. A 8. D 9. B 10. B 11. B 12. D 13. D 14. D 15. A

Test 81 PART A. 1. People planning to move to Florida usually do so because of the mild climate. 2. While driving through the Ocala National Forest [*or* Driving through the Ocala National Forest],

I was a bear. 3. Runes, a form of writing used in ancient times, are often associated with magic and mystery. 4. After robbing Mrs. Grant's house, the two men stole her car and led the plice on a high-speed chase. 5. The car stolen last night was a black 2004 Ford Explorer with tinted windows. 6. For the party, let's use the crystal goblets on the top shelf 7. They didn't enjoy their summertime visit to the Florida Keys because of the hot, humid weather 8. The salesperson earning the most in commissions this month will get a bonus. 9. Despite being an hour late, Eric expected his date to be there waiting. 10. The Statue of Liberty, located in New York Harbor, was a welcoming sight to the immigrants who arrived by ship in the early 1900s. PART B. Answers will vary but should contain an appositive and be a complete sentence.

Test 82 PART A. 1. The dress in the store window is expensive. 2. The reporter on TV right now is a veteran. 3. The sofa in our living room needs to be replaced. 4. The astronaut famous for being the first man on the moon is Neil Armstrong. 5. Bill Gates, one of the founders of Microsoft, is extraordinarily wealthy. 6. Sorrento, the town where my grandfather was born, is in southern Italy. 7. The car damaged in the accident is still on the side of the road. 8. The person elected president has huge responsibilities. 9. The cake sitting on the counter is for tonight's dinner guests. 10. The people running the bakery have decided to close the shop on Sundays. PART B. 1. X, who were at the meeting 2. X, a soft 3. X, built in 1886 4. C 5. C 6. X, Being hungry [or Because he was hungry] 7. C 8. C 9. C 10. X, everything that is worth $500 [or everything worth $500] PART C. 1. While attending college, Kim is holding down a full-time job. 2. When tired, I find that I can't concentrate on anything. 3. While studying for her test, Cindy realized that she had left out some material. 4. After being robbed, Don had to file a police report. 5. After finding her luggage, Edna walked toward the airport parking lot. 6. When in trouble, dial 9-1-1. 7. When confused about a grammar point, Janet asks her teacher for help. 8. While eating, my dog will snap at anyone who approaches him. 9. When notified about jury duty, I reported to the courthouse to sign up. 10. When at the beach, you should use plenty of sunscreen.

Test 83 PART A. 1. shouldn't have . . . could have . . . would have 2. should have . . . could/might have . . . would have 3. could/might have . . . couldn't/can't have . . . must have 4. should have . . . could have, wouldn't have PART B. 1. were able to 2. couldn't/wasn't able to 3. was able to 4. could/was able to 5. was able to PART C. 1. use to be 2. used to play 3. used to/would hide 4. would open 5. would yell 6. used to/would sneak 7. would laugh 8. used to torture PART D. Answers will vary but should use correct past modal 1. a. I had to . . . b. I didn't have to 2. I was going to . . . but . . . 3. I was going to/supposed to . . . , but . . .

Test 84 PART A. 1. D 2. F 3. I 4. A 5. H 6. B 7. J 8. E 9. C 10. G PART B. 1. C 2. D 3. B 4. D 5. A 6. C 7. D 8. B 9. A 10. C PART C. 1. X, couldn't whistle 2. C 3. X, may have left [or might have left] 4. C 5. C 6. C 7. C 8. X, must have driven 9. X, is supposed to start 10. X, is going [or is going to go]

Test 85 PART A. everyone, the United States, the team, dancing, each of the students, traffic, the furniture, the news, politics, all of the money, the newspaper PART B. 1. was 2. are 3. have 4. is bringing 5. was 6. takes 7. are 8. is 9. offers 10. speak 11. is 12. is 13. have 14. are 15. are 16. is 17. is 18. work 19. arrives 20. are

Test 86 PART A. 1. makes 2. increases 3. are going 4. has worked 5. ought to come 6. can help 7. is 8. Is 9. agree 10. has been PART B. 1. A 2. B 3. C 4. C 5. D 6. A 7. C 8. C 9. A 10. B PART C. 1. play 2. was 3. was 4. will keep 5. has 6. Do 7. has 8. knows 9. have 10. should

Test 87 PART A. 1. underlined anniversary of wedding (wedding anniversary) 2. looked for (at) 3. at (in) Key West 4. on a little church (in) 5. in (on) Simonton Street 6. in (on) Feb. 17 7. on (in) her white dress 8. on (in) her hands 9. white roses' bouquet (bouquet of white roses) 10. looked for (at) 11. full from (of) love 12. at (on) each other's 13. out from (of) 14. rice in (at/on) them 15. looking forward for (to) 16. married with (to) 17. surprise to (for) them PART B. Answers will vary but should be logical and contain correct preposition. 1. We communicate by e-mail. 2. They eat with chopsticks. 3. I usually get up at 7. 4. I would rather live in a big city. 5. I'm proud of my career. 6. I keep important documents in a safe. 7. My favorite program is at 10 P.M. on Fridays. 8. I would like to live in Italy.

Test 88 PART A. 1. at . . . on 2. in 3. in 4. up . . . out 5. by 6. to 7. with 8. In order to 9. of 10. in . . . of 11. to 12. to 13. at 14. for 15. up PART B. 1. B 2. C 3. D 4. D 5. A 6. D 7. C 8. A 9. B 10. A 11. B 12. C 13. D 14. B 15. A

Test 89 1. were 2. had 3. are 4. has concluded 5. met 6. is 7. tried 8. was 9. varies 10. was

Test 90 1. works 2. must be 3. are 4. drowned 5. believe 6. is 7. attempted 8. consist 9. insist 10. lasted

Test 91 PART A. Word endings are shown here; sentences will vary. 1. colorful 2. dangerous 3. worker 4. completely 5. happiness 6. darken 7. understandable 8. performance 9. artist 10. finalize PART B. 1. By the time Alberto was 30, he had lived in 15 different countries. 2. A month before summer officially started, the temperature had already been in the 90s every day. 3. When Scott got to the party at midnight, almost everyone had gone home. 4. Just before we arrived at the beach ready to swim, someone had spotted a shark. 5. Nelson Mandela had been a civil rights activist and a political prisoner before he became President of South Africa. PART C. 1. containing 2. had told . . . would have 3. the principal's office is 4. lead-

ing . . . are 5. lives 6. that . . . won . . . would
7. was . . . what 8. must have . . . off 9. on . . .
of . . . while 10. were . . . would . . . rated 11. is
. . . Are 12. were . . . about . . . had paid . . .
wouldn't have 13. Whether . . . have 14. qualifying
15. When . . . were . . . use to

Test 92 PART A. 1. had arrived 2. hadn't had
3. musician 4. curly 5. will assume 6. had 7. had
. . . could have 8. Before 9. that 10. even if
11. that 12. what 13. may have 14. wasn't able to
15. Given that 16. are 17. are 18. with 19. to
20. of PART B. 1. C 2. C 3. X, had slept 4. X, had
not finished 5. X, discussion 6. C 7. X, will be
8. X, were 9. X, ought to have 10. C 11. X, despite
the fact 12. C 13. C 14. X, where the jewelry
department is 15. C PART C. 1. B 2. A 3. C 4. D
5. B 6. C 7. A 8. C 9. B 10. C 11. B 12. D 13. B
14. A 15. A

Test 93 1. dumping → dumped 2. than → as
3. exaggerate → exaggerated 4. cloths → clothes
5. museum → museums 6. requires → is required
7. in north → in the northern 8. has → ø 9. was
→ ø 10. response → responses

Test 94 1. another → other 2. an earliest → earlier
[or an earliest → his earliest] 3. it's → its 4. than
→ as 5. many → much 6. destinations → destination 7. I → me 8. taken → took [or taken → have
taken] 9. will → ø 10. for → about

Test 95 1. like → alike 2. became → has become [or
is becoming or will become] 3. increase → increasing 4. pass → have passed 5. none → no 6. estimating → estimated 7. a statue bronze → a bronze
statue 8. there → it 9. aluminum small → small

aluminum 10. was first → was the first

Test 96 1. was → ø 2. all the → all 3. few → little
4. neighbor's → neighbors 5. that → as 6. needed
→ need 7. total score → a total score 8. good →
goods 9. Afterward Laos → After Laos
10. returned his → returned to his

Test 97 1. did → done 2. must to show → must
show 3. suggestion → suggests 4. so → more
5. Alike → Like 6. mental → mentally 7. will have
→ had 8. did → was 9. Comparing → Compared
10. begun → began

Test 98 1. when was → when he was 2. choice →
chosen [or the choice or a choice] 3. well → good
4. these → this 5. possibly → possible 6. none →
no 7. its → it 8. promoting → promote 9. live →
living [or live → life] 10. winning → won

Test 99 1. most → ø 2. resident → residential
3. strong → strengthen 4. less → fewer 5. differ →
differs 6. most easiest → easiest 7. have → had
8. any → no 9. today it → today 10. member →
members

Test 100 1. Afterward → After 2. none → no
3. eating → eaten 4. an → a 5. change → chang-
ing 6. they → ø 7. victim said → victim is said
8. In spite a wealth → In spite of a wealth 9. successful → were successful 10. many → much

Test 101 1. decide → decision 2. go to the office →
going to the office 3. Some choice → Some choose
4. Alike hurricanes → Like hurricanes 5. amount
of homeworks → amount of homework 6. to score
→ scoring 7. to destroy → destroying 8. required
→ are required 9. most easiest → easiest 10. a
number of fact → a number of facts

Test Index

Numbers refer to test numbers, not page numbers.